CHRISTIANITY AND MARXISM

Edited by

Alan Scarfe and Patrick Sookhdeo

CHRISTIANITY AND MARXISM

Editors

Alan Scarfe
and
Patrick Sookhdeo

EXETER
THE PATERNOSTER PRESS

Copyright © The Paternoster Press Ltd., 1982

AUSTRALIA
*Bookhouse Australia Ltd.,
P.O. Box 115, Flemington Markets,
NSW 2129*

SOUTH AFRICA
*Oxford University Press,
P.O. Box 1141,
Cape Town*

British Library Cataloguing in Publication Data

Christianity & Marxism.
  1. Communism and Christianity
  I. Scarfe, Alan II. Sookhdeo, Patrick
  200   HX536

ISBN 0-85364-289-3

*Typeset by Photo-Graphics, Yarcombe and printed and
bound in Great Britain at The Pitman Press, Bath for the
Paternoster Press Ltd., Paternoster House, 3 Mount Rad-
ford Crescent, Exeter, Devon.*

Contents

Introduction

Perhaps the greatest single challenge confronting the church today is Marxism. The past fifty years have seen the advance of Marxism world wide. Sections of Asia, Africa, Europe, South America have all come under its sway. The 1948 Lambeth Conference stated that the 'supreme conflict of our generation is a struggle between the Christian and the Marxist for the soul of man'.

Marxism presents to many an attractive alternative to the type of society which has produced injustice and poverty. John Pierce puts it succinctly:

> The Communist Party offers its members an organization to belong to, a measure of comradeship and protection and a cause to be committed to. To the idealist it offers a promise of a world free from injustice, war and poverty.
>
> To the destitute it offers a promise of material possession. To the victims of injustice it offers a chance to get revenge. To the intellectual it offers a philosophy which explains why things are the way they are and how to change them.

The essence of Marxist philosophy is that theory and practice is seen as an integrated whole. The dichotomy between faith and practice, all too prevalent within Christianity finds little expression in Marxism. The Marxist analysis of life, with its humanist, materialist foundation seeks not just to analyse causes but to suggest and implement remedies. It would be easy to write off Marxism as irrelevant in the social political and economic arena or as simply demonic in the religious sphere, but this would be naive. The issues confronting the Christian Church in its relationships with Marxism are complex. On the one hand the Christian would not want to reject every tenet of Marxism, from which he can learn much, but on the other there is much that he would disclaim.

The Christian can learn from the underlying unity that exists within Marxism. Marxism is seen essentially as a whole, although made up of a number of components; it therefore sees the world in global terms. It is interesting to note that in Marxist countries where Christians have lost the freedom to divide, in many instances they have been forced to work together. The church desperately needs unity. This unity must be not just external, but organic, a unity that will span the centres of division and will present to the world the church, Christ's visible body on the earth.

Christians can learn from the Marxist concern for society, a concern that is aimed at the transformation of society, the rooting out of fear, oppression and injustice. The Christian in considering his concern for the structures of society is brought to realize that the gospel speaks not just to the individual but also to society. God's concern is for man in community. The gospel therefore has to speak to the unjust structures that imprison men and women within their walls.

The Marxist desire is for a new order, an earthly utopia, where a reconstituted world will amply provide for the needs of men, where justice and equity will reign. The gospel however, is essentially the gospel of the kingdom; it is a kingdom that is within as well as around. It is both spiritual and material. It is both visible and tangible; it is both present and future. It is the reign of God over the individual, the church and ultimately the whole of creation, culminating in a new heaven and earth. The Christian therefore works for a new society not built upon humanist ideals but upon the principle of divine intervention. God not only acts in history, but works through his Spirit in every facet of society. The new age for which the Christian looks is already here in that it has been inaugurated by Christ's first coming. His second coming will establish it by sweeping away all sin, greed and corruption, when his people shall inhabit the earth.

The Marxist is motivated by a sense of mission to gain control and finally to rule. His desire is to capture the mind, to transform society and ultimately the nations of this world with his own philosophy. It is a mission that is dynamic and imperative for him. In many instances it is costly. It forms the motivating force of his life and affects his relationship with his family, his friends and those with whom he works. Everything he sees or reads is dictated by a fundamental thought, that Marxism is right, that it has the capacity to solve the world's problems.

Similarly, the Church needs a sense of mission; it needs to be motivated afresh by the impetus of the Holy Spirit. It needs to recognize again that it holds the key to the understanding of the world and to the way it can be transformed. It needs afresh a vision to see the impossible achieved; it needs the courage to face the cost of such involvement. The flabby, materialistic, individualistic, moribund Christianity that surrounds us is far from the gospel of Jesus Christ.

The churches' identification with the power structures has resulted in a loss of credibility. The churches' identification with the affluent and prosperous has resulted in a loss of relevancy. She is seen as having little to say to the sort of world that is so desperately in need. She is seen to be lacking in compassion, lacking in true involvement, lacking in the cross. Yet this is the very point at which Christianity can speak so aptly to Marxism.

The Christian cannot only affirm the good within Marxism but also in observing its weaknesses can point beyond it. Marxism rests its hope in man. It denies the supernatural. It has dispensed with God. The Christian in affirming the authority of God and the reality of the spiritual realm is saying that there is more to man than meets the eye. The conception of Marxism with man at the helm of his destiny is an unworkable concept for it fails to take into account selfishness, greed, anger, hatred.

The only hope of a better society is a better man. Only the

new man created in Christ can herald in Christ's new age. Any scheme therefore which seeks to reconstruct society while ignoring the redemption of the individual is unthinkable. Alternatively, any effort which seeks only to save people from their sins without transforming them into a movement which eradicates the evils of society is equally unthinkable.

The call to the church in its encounter with Marxism is not to react or retreat in fear, but to give itself in loving service to the Marxist. This must involve compassion not condemnation; it will go on to an accurate study of the underlying principles of the system of philosophy which controls the lives and destinies of multitudes, and will not be content in making generalized assumptions founded upon emotion rather than fact. Finally those who have begun to feel and to understand something of the nature of Marxism must continue to rest upon the truth, once for all received, the truth of the Bible.

It is hoped that this symposium will go some way towards helping in the understanding and assessment of Marxism, and also in the approach to the Marxist, both on an intellectual and a personal level.

1

Marxism: The Twentieth Century Religion

GEORGE PATERSON

Definition of Religion

There is no doubt that Marxism, which set out to discredit and even to destroy institutional religion — and it is important to emphasize the 'institutional' for reasons which will become evident — has itself become an institutional religion in the twentieth century, with all of the weaknesses and few of the strengths of the historical religious institutions.

It is necessary in making such a sweeping assertion to make it clear at the beginning what constitutes a proper definition of 'religion', for it is one of those words that everyone — from the eponymous man-in-the-street to the ubiquitous pontificators-in-the-media uses with idiosyncratic assurance, often with cavalier effrontery, but with little specific relevance to its actual meaning.

The *Concise Oxford Dictionary* gives several meanings to the word:

(i) Monastic condition, being monk or nun;
(ii) One of the prevalent systems of faith and worship;
(iii) Practice of sacred rites;
(iv) Human recognition of superhuman controlling power and especially of a personal God entitled to obedi-

ence; effect of such recognition on conduct and mental
attitude;

(v)   Action that one is bound to do.

Number (i) might be excluded from the general definition
of Marxism as a religion, although examples of vocational
dedication could be given to support this, — as, for example,
the five 'orders' of China's 'Red Guards' — but numbers (ii),
(iii), (iv) and (v) provide an adequate starting point for the
assertion that Marxism in one form or another can be now
justifiably termed a religion. Any objection to the use of the
word 'sacred' in (iii) can be met by pointing out that this word
means more than something simply consecrated to a deity,
and may be legitimately applied to something dedicated or
appropriated or reserved to some person or purpose, or to
something safeguarded by tradition as well as religion,
something regarded as inviolable. Further, the Marxist recognition of a supernatural controlling power (iv), while not
attributed to a personal God, is certainly attributed to certain
'laws' that determine history (e.g. 'the law of motion in
history'), and obedience to those laws is demanded.

However, in studying religions more than simple con-
formity to dictionary definitions is required, and several
other criteria are usually observed. There are the more
obvious external aspects, rituals, customs, buildings, books,
etc; then there are the doctrines, the ideas and beliefs, from
which all external practices are derived; finally, there are the
existential, or experiential, aspects so fundamental to the
believers of each religion and without which all other
phenomena would disappear.

These three fundamental criteria have been expanded in a
recent study[1] by Ninian Smart of Lancaster University, to
form an excellent phenomenological framework for the study
of religion:

(i)   *Doctrinal:* Most religions have official teaching or
       doctrines.

(ii)   *Mythological:* Religions express their beliefs in story
       form, sometimes historical events, sometimes fiction-
       al or parable stories with symbolic meaning.

(iii) *Ethical:* Religions prescribe principles and sometimes codes of moral conduct, related to (i) and (ii).

(iv) *Ritual:* All specifically religious actions, from sacramental observance, to genuflecting, to telling beads, to use of language.

(v) *Experiential:* Religious faith is founded upon, and sustained by, intuitive insight, as, for example, the conversion of St. Paul, or the enlightenment of the Buddha, or the illuminative experience of the ordinary believer, leading to fundamental change.

(vi) *Social:* Religion requires the association of fellow-believers in groups for its expansion and perpetuation.

These six 'dimensions of religion' are interrelated and interdependent and, together with the *Concise Oxford Dictionary* definitions, provide an adequate modality for the examination of Marxism as a religion in the essay that follows.

Historical Setting of the Marxist Revolution

Despite appearances — and even assertions — the Marxist revolution is a twentieth and not a nineteenth-century phenomenon. The birth of modern democracy took place in the second half of the eighteenth century, and was the result of a spiritual and not a political or social revolution. The importance of this cannot be too strongly emphasised, not only for a proper understanding of Marxism but also to explain the subsequent deterioration of a Secular Democracy bereft of spiritual content because of the compromised betrayal of the discredited institutional religions of the West, Catholic and Protestant, leaving a vacuum which both wings of the Christian Church failed to fill but which Marxism successfully exploited.

In his book, *The Gods of Revolution*[2], writing on the subject of the English, French and American Revolutions, Christopher Dawson has a chapter entitled 'The Birth of Democracy', in which he says, 'This (European Enlightenment) movement was not originally a democratic one and it was only in the second half of the eighteenth century that the democratic ideal was clearly formulated.' Then, going on to speak of Jean-Jacques Rousseau as the real force behind the French Revolution, and not the usually accepted Voltaire or Diderot, he declares:

> It was he who first fired men's minds with the ideal of democracy not as a mere system of government *but as a new way of life, a vision of social justice and fraternity which is nothing else than the kingdom of God on earth*. It is true that Rousseau himself was not a revolutionary in the ordinary sense. The revolution that he preached was not a political or an economic one *but a spiritual one*... (my italics).

But the Christian Church in the eighteenth century, both Catholic and Protestant, was in no state to deal with the variety of social and political issues being raised, because of their own internal squabbles, jealousies and rivalries, and it was left to the Jacobin Society, led by the formidable Robespierre, to emerge as the 'spiritual' leader of France following on the Revolution. The Jacobins were the vital dynamic power behind the political mechanism and under Robespierre's driving leadership — he too regarded the Revolution as essentially a moral and religious reformation — they sought to fill the gap left by the guilty Churches.

At the mammoth Festival in Paris on 6 June, 1794, to launch the new radical religious movement, 'The Worship of the Supreme Being', Robespierre himself 'officiated as a kind of priest', and said:[3]

> Is it not He Who from the beginning of time had decreed the Republic and has ordained for all ages and for all peoples, liberty, good faith and justice?
> He has not created kings to devour the human race: He has not created priests to harness us to the chariot of kings and to give the world an example of baseness and perfidy and falsehood, but he has created the universe to manifest His power: He has created men to help each other, to love one another and to attain happiness by the way of virtue...

Yet Robespierre himself came to be regarded as the representative and embodiment of the terrorist dictatorship, the fanatical 'any means at any cost' advocate which was the cause of the destruction of the government and revolution. With the Christian churches in disarray, and the 'popular religion' discredited, developing democracy became secularized in the West and had less and less recourse to religious representatives except on ceremonial occasions. So just as modern secular democracy was being born institutional Christianity was entering its terminal stage.

The significance of these events at this time was noted and emphasised by W.F. Wertheim, in his book,[4] *Evolution and Revolution*:

> Evidently, in order to atract broad masses, a revolution needed elements of popular cultism that had hitherto been associated with religion.
>
> In later revolutions there were similar experiences. One could quote in this connection the Lenin cult in the Mausoleum on the Red Square in Moscow, or certain facets of the Mao cult in China today.
>
> Evidently, the kind of fervour earlier associated with religious movements seeks expression in familiar forms even though the prevalent revolutionary ideology is a-religious or anti-religious as, for example, the branding of religion by classical Marxism as 'Opiate of the People'. Each revolutionary movement, though rational in its means and immediate political aims, represents, at the same time, the dream of a fully renewed social order, and this dream may find expression in quasi-religious forms...

Following on the French Revolution of 1789 there were the revolutions of 1830, 1848 and 1871, passing from the purely political to the social and then to the socialist. These were followed by the technological revolution, which began with the English Industrial Revolution and gradually extended into continental Europe. This in turn produced profound social changes, and the sudden change in the internal balance of power, and the vast increase in wealth and opportunity, set up a process of intense competition and social tension between individuals.

This was the world into which Karl Heinrich Marx was born on May 5, 1818, offspring of a long line of Rabbis and son of a solicitor who had adopted Christianity the year before

Karl was born. He attended a Jesuit school at Trier in Germany for a period of five years, and went on to read jurisprudence, philosophy and history at Bonn and Berlin Universities. Thus the scene was set for Marx's theories of a moral solution for an immoral society, as well as an historical necessity. 'Original sin is everywhere at work,' he declared in *Das Capital*.

The young Marx was concerned with values, with high ideals, rather than inflexible economic forces. He criticised the French Revolution for having produced only political emancipation and not a 'human emancipation'. The Revolution had given political freedom to the individual, but had not made him a true human being who would live as a brother with his fellow man. It had created liberty, but not fraternity. Man still had to be freed from the bondage of his own inhumanity, delivered from his egotism, and Marx even quoted Rousseau as saying that the task was nothing less than the changing of human nature: to put responsibility in the place of mere independence. This 'new man' would have to put his inherent selfishness behind and put the interests of humanity before his own.

Whether Marx planned it or not with this object in view, sooner or later, he or his disciples would found an organisation that given time, opportunity, books, vision and ambition, would become an institutional religion to change individuals whose purpose would be to change the world. Where Marx broke with other philosophies was in this emphasis on action rather than theorising. In his Eleventh Thesis on Feuerbach he laid down his famous axiom: 'The philosophers have only interpreted the world: the point, however, is to change it.'

C. Wright Mills, writing in his book,[5] *The Marxists*, describes the difference between Marx and other social scientists:

> The social scientists study the details of small-scale milieus; Marx studied such details, too, but always within the structure of a total society. The social scientists, knowing little history, study short-run trends; Marx, using historical materials with superb mastery, takes as his unit of study entire epochs. The values of

the social scientists generally lead them to accept their society pretty much as it is; the values of Marx lead him to condemn his society — root, stock and branch. The social scientists see society's problems as matters only of 'disorganization'; Marx sees problems as inherent contradictions in the existing structure. The social scientists see their society continuing in an evolutionary way without qualitative breaks in its structure; Marx sees in the future of this society a qualitative break: a new form of society — in fact a new epoch — is going to come about by means of revolution.'

And R.H. Tawney compared Marx with Calvin in his sense of vision and destiny:[6]

It is not wholly fanciful to say that, on a narrower stage but with not less formidable weapons, Calvin did for the *bourgeoisie* of the sixteenth century what Marx did for the proletariat of the nineteenth, or that the doctrine of Predestination satisfied the same hunger for an assurance that the forces of the Universe are on the side of the Elect as was to be assuaged in a different age by the theory of Historical Materialism. He... taught them to feel that they were a Chosen People, made them conscious of their great destiny in the Providential plan and resolute to realize it.

Marx's 'Spiritual' Ideas

Marxism, like Christianity, claims to be a philosophy of life for transforming the world. Marx's *Weltanschauung der Welveranderung* means literally 'world outlook' or 'philosophy of life', and 'world change' or 'transforming the world'. Marx possibly developed the thesis originated by Bacon and Descartes, that it is possible to know nature and to use this knowledge in such a way as to master and change nature, to postulate that human history is not a meaningless and accidental sequence of events: that there were laws of social development which could be discovered and taken into account, and whose realisation could even be speeded up on the basis of that knowledge.

But the inherent contradiction at the core of this postulation was not solved by Marx in his lifetime, nor by his followers since. How is it possible to transfer a thesis appropriate to the natural sciences and apply it to the study of society, which deals with men and women, with active individuals endowed with consciousness and will? However, Marx went ahead anyway and, with Engels, taught a world outlook of changing the world, the conception of being able to have a powerful influence upon events through understanding their inter-connections in history. From this they deduced among other 'laws' the 'law of motion in history', by which they explained the succession of various forms of society and the rhythms of this succession: as, for example, feudalism to capitalism to socialism. Out of this revelation of Historical Materialism Marx forced an institutional instrument to save the world from superstition and sin.

The socio-political philosophy deriving from this fundamental concept is now loosely called 'Marxism', 'Marxist-Leninism', 'Communism', 'Socialist Democracy' after the various followers of Marx. To these has been added in the past three decades the term 'Maoism', after the unique form developed in China by Mao Tsetung.

Marx's early vision was to turn men and women, reduced to empty individuality, away from their purely private interests and preoccupations, and to unite them with a community based on freedom rather than the dominance of a few. Even the religious views of the young Marx — a disillusioned product of a Christian theological college — were different from his later attitudes and history's interpretation of them. Marx's oft-quoted, 'Religion is the opium of the people', is a gross misquotation, taken out of context. What he actually said was that institutional religion is a perverted consciousness of the world, arising because the society which produced it is perverted:

> Religion is the sob of the oppressed creature, the heart of a heartless world, the spirit of conditions utterly unspiritual. It is the opiate of the people ... The criticism of Religion is the premise of all criticism ... a criticism of the vale of misery ... The removal of Religion as the illusory happiness of the people means the demand of the people for their real happiness.

Marx did not consider religion itself the root of all evil; the radical defect, not the sinful inheritance, of mankind.

Criticism of religion was meaningful only in the setting of social criticism. Professor Jan Lochman, the Czechoslovak theologian, in his book *Encountering Marx*,[7] has emphasized this widely misunderstood aspect of Marxism:

> It is important to establish which religions and ecclesiastical manifestations of religion are the target of Marx's attack. It is my assessment that his protest is mainly against two phenomena: the misuse of political power by Christendom, and the worship of mammon in the religion of the time...
>
> With clear reference to the biblical message, which the 'Christian State' should certainly have taken seriously, he described emphatically how 'the infamy of its secular aims, which religion covers with sanctity, and the glory of its religious consciousness, are in unresolved conflict.' This he establishes in a way that should have come from the pen of a learned divine of the time ...'(pp. 83–4).

'Christian Marxists' in Eastern Europe and Latin America are aware of many of the early Marx's 'spiritual' concepts and valid objections to religious institutions and this accounts for the creative dialogue now taking place in these countries. Milan Machovec, a Czech Marxist and Professor of Philosophy at the University of Prague from 1953 to 1970, has written a remarkable book, *A Marxist Looks at Jesus*, a scholarly examination of Christianity in history, in which he describes a part of this dialogue:

> In the heritage of classical Marxism, and also in modern Marxism when it has not betrayed its heritage, the historical-materialist methodology is of much greater importance. One of its most elementary principles is the teaching that developments and transformations in the realm of human 'spirit' and 'mind' — which give rise to political, moral and religious ideas and other ideas with a historical origin — are ultimately explicable by the developments, contradictions, interests and changes that take place in the socio-economic infra-structure ...
>
> Now what does all this mean in practice and in relation to the principal positions of Christianity? How does it affect Jesus' uniqueness and central messianic role for all humanity? Marx could admire Jesus' love of children, Kautsky the revolutionary and utopian-communistic tendencies in early Christianity,

modern Marxists can be inspired by particular biblical episodes, but every Marxist, even the most 'modern' ... has taken over this method from Marx as a 'classical inheritance' ... (p.22).

Marx's New Social Order

An important emphasis in Marx's 'philosophy of man' is his doctrine of 'alienation'. It was the importance of this problem of 'the alienation of man', in Marx's view, which led him to break with the dialectical limitations of Feuerbach. Feuerbach, in the tradition of Hegel, argued that self-alienation consists of the temptation of (religious) man to project his wishes and longings to an imaginary concept of God, thus developing a 'fetishist' tendency. But Marx went far beyond this, and it is very significant that his most important thinking on the subject of man in society came to public notice only in 1932, ninety years after he committed his theories to paper.

As a young man, in 1844, during his exile in Paris, he wrote *Economic and Philosophical Manuscripts*. For whatever reason — perhaps because they were at odds with the prevailing Stalinist tendencies during that period — they remained relatively unknown until they appeared in a Czech translation in 1961.

Marx's image of man is one which involves 'the place of man in the universe', and this place is determined by his labour which binds him to nature. It is in man's labour that he and the world of nature achieve a common purpose; through which, by extension of this thinking, the concept of God is eliminated:

> Once the essential reality of man in nature, man as the existence of nature for man, and nature for man as the existence of man, has become evident in practical life and sense experience, then the question of an alien being, of a being above nature and above man — a question that implies an admission of the unreality of nature and man — has become impossible in practice ...[8]

Thus, labour, according to Marx, makes God superfluous. But in the process of consolidating his thesis Marx has then to go on and lay down his own alternative doctrine of replacing a personal God with impersonal laws: the solution to the mystery of the world's history, labour as 'redemption' of man and nature, labour as the instrument of salvation in the universe of man. Labour is 'the confirmation of man as a conscious species-being', making him different from other beings, other creatures. Man produces not only out of necessity, but also out of freedom 'fashions things according to the laws of beauty' (op. cit. pp. 139–40).

But labour is not only a theory of free, creative, beautiful activity; it is also compulsion, exploitation, oppression, poverty, weariness and deprivation. It is demeaning and threatening to humanity; and this aspect is defined: 'Work is alienation'.

'The object that labour produces, its product, confronts it as an alien being, as a power independent of the producer.'

So Marx, having eliminated a personal God requiring faith and works for salvation of the individual, postulated a theory of 'good works' leading to communism and salvation and 'evil works' leading to capitalism and domination.

Work, according to Marx, is the setting for a true humanity, and alienated labour strikes at the root of meaningful life. The very nature of man becomes perverted by this alienation, since a perverted system of production necessarily produces perverted human relations. Human self-alienation was exemplified and exacerbated by private property so this would have to be abolished to restore 'the human essence by and for man'.

Describing this in his book, *Encountering Marx: Bonds and Barriers Between Christians and Marxists*, Professor Jan Lochman says:

In these words the wide horizon of communism as understood by Marx is most clearly and unequivocally expressed. In the communist society we are concerned not with some new step in the social and historical development of man, but with a radical leap forward, which is qualitatively new in world history. With it the 'Babylonian captivity' of alienation is smashed and overcome. The great Exodus out of the 'kingdom of necessity' into the 'kingdom of freedom' has taken place, the new redeemed world has arrived.

The beginnings of this new world are simple and clear to describe: they are measured by the overcoming of private property. This, according to Marx, corresponds to the logic of history. As the various levels of alienation arose because of the coming of private property, so the process of redemption is by way of the abolition of private property. With the fall of this 'evil enemy', the way lies open for the creation of freedom for man. This is not only in the economic field but in every important human activity... (p. 63).

This destruction of the power of private property, the power of capital, with its consequent removal of human self-alienation then made possible the humanizing of the working process, and as Marx and Engels described in *German Ideology* in 1845 — in utopian millennial terminology:

> ... to do this today, that tomorrow; to hunt in the morning; afternoon to fish; evening to look after the cattle; after eating to criticise, as I wish; without becoming a hunter, or a shepherd, or a critic.

The death blow to capital in the abolition of private property would restore inter-personal relations between men and women. The cultural alienation of religion and ideologies would disappear (including the opposition between materialism and idealism); also, political alienation in the state and the alienation of the nuclear family.

This new humanity in new 'fellowship' groups in a new society Marx saw in embryonic form during a visit to Paris:

> When the communist workers come together, it is first of all for teaching, propaganda, etc., but at the same time there is evident a natural need, a need for company, and so the means becomes a purpose. This practical movement can be seen in its most brilliant form by observing the French *ouvriers* together. Smoking, drinking, eating, etc., are no longer means for bringing them together, or social methods. The company, the coming together, the entertainment, which again has fellowship for its purpose, takes them over. The brotherhood of man is no mere slogan, but is the truth with them. The jewel of humanity shines upon us as we see these forms, hardened by work, coming together.[9]

This is still the ideal of a truly Marxist society in the twentieth century, as demonstrated in a recent article in *The Times*[10] on the subject of China:

> A Communist Party functionary was recently telling a foreigner how Chinese society ideally should be organised. Everyone, he said, should live in the compound where he works. If for some reason the workplace and the home must be in different locations, he said, then people should still live in the same place as their workmates.
>
> The worker who commutes between home and job poses a problem, the party member said. He can be two different men. At the factory his political attitudes and work habits are known, but the party would not know how he acts around the home. The party functionary said it would be a healthier political situation for the man to be among his fellow-workers 24 hours a day...'

The Chinese concept of revolutionary Marxism is much more advanced than that of any other communist society in the twentieth century, absorbing every aspect of life — games, books, art, science, drama, music, the media, and, most of all, the education and indoctrination of children. (See under 'The Spiritual Marxism of Mao Tse-tung'.) This religion-like conditioning has been described in a report in *New Internationalist*,[11] based on a study tour of Chinese homes, kindergartens and schools by thirteen distinguished American child-care specialists:

> The Chinese leadership has decided what kind of society it wants and what values and attitudes are necessary among the people to create and preserve that society. In common with other Marxists they believe that the environment alone shapes the personality and therefore their education and child-care systems are explicitly designed to create the values and attitudes demanded by their social and political goals.
>
> Like any good Jesuit, they begin with the very young child. At around the time when children in the West are being introduced to Jesus, the Bible and the long donkey-ride to Bethlehem, the Chinese child is being introduced to Mao Tse-tung, the Little Red Book and the Long March. At about the age of two the Chinese toddler sees the large colourful posters of Mao and his thoughts. Soon afterwards, he or she begins to hear, for a few

minutes each day, the story of revolutionary heroes like Lei Feng
and the values they personify.

Slowly, as the nursery school child learns to hold crayons,
name common objects, and follow simple hygiene rituals, he or
she also begins to be weaned on to the solid food of communist
ideology. Side by side with the three R's the Chinese child also
begins to learn the Five Loves — Chairman Mao, Workers-
Peasants-Soldiers, the Communist Party, the Great Socialist
Motherland and Physical Labour.

Marx and Engels were aware of a whole series of important
parallels between the situation, ideals and development of
early Christianity and those of the socialist movement in
their own time, with Marx more cautious in his analyses than
Engels, combining the vision of the Communist future with
scientific analysis. Professor Milan Machovec, in describing
this development, says:

> When, however, in the twentieth century many analogies
> between the two movements became apparent to socialist and
> also to non-socialist intellectuals, and as the archetypes of social
> events and great personalities were studied, the idea began to
> grow that perhaps Marx himself represented a 'prophetic type'
> who in some sense would fulfil in future ages a complex, great
> and multifarious mission and role comparable with that of the
> Master from Galilee (Lowith, Popper, Kunzli)... (p. 216)

Marx, therefore, was not against religion *per se* but against
a perverted institutional religion arising out of a perverted
society. In a utopian Marxist society this perverted institutional religion would naturally wither away to be replaced by
the Marxist 'new men and women'.

Men and women were imperfect, fragmented, disfigured,
and incapable of transforming themselves, said Marx. But the
more they were able to appropriate 'human reality' in all its
forms, through the spirit as well as the senses and the
intelligence, the greater was the possibility of being 'whole'.
Marx was concerned with building up, not with destruction;
with healing, not with disease.

The early Marx was concerned with men and women
loving, rather than having; with caring, rather than getting.

Speaking of 'the whole man', the 'man endowed with all the senses', and the realising of his place in society by 'appropriation', he saw love as an essential form of such appropriation. But in a world given over to the pursuit and possession of things, to commerce and profit, the creative human act of loving had shrivelled into the mere sterile act of 'having', which saw the immediate physical possession as 'the unique goal of life and existence'. This mentality had infected love itself, twisting the relationship between men and women into a relationship of ownership and domination, debasing it into a 'thing'.

These high ideals were the kind of prophetic vision of a coming order of Marxist society for the realisation of which men and women were prepared to die, and which called forth the shrewd observation in the Report of the Lambeth Conference in 1948:

> No presentation of the Christian world-view can command the assent of the rising generation unless it has squarely come to grips with the dogmas of Dialectical Materialism. For Marxism, by an ironic paradox, is at some points nearer to the Christian doctrine than any other philosophy, and this makes its rivalry all the more formidable.

The Marxist Experience

A central tenet of Marxist doctrine, never lost in theory over the years and throughout different communist administrations but certainly ignored in practice, is the *experiential* necessity for the 'new man' in a truly Marxist society. At the important 22nd Party Congress of the CPUSSR 1961 the creation of the 'new man' was placed high on the list of the ideological tasks of the Party:

> *The Party regards the education of the new man as the most difficult task in the communist reshaping of society.* Until we remove bourgeois moral principles roots and all, train men in the spirit of communist morality *and renew them spiritually and morally, it will not be possible to build a communist society'* (my italics).

Here we have a spiritual change in man regarded as decisive, and placed *ahead* of the utopian communist final change of the structures of society — and before the abolishing of compulsory work. According to Marx the communist society of the future can only be made possible by a high rate of productivity that can no longer be obtained by other 'outward' norms, coercion or incentives, *but only through the spontaneous efforts of a selfless, conscientious 'new man' acting from an inner conviction.* In other words, without the changed 'new man' there can be no communism in the true sense of the word. The success of Marxism, therefore, depends upon the primary conversion of the individual into a 'new man' — just as Christianity requires being 'born again' into a 'new creature'.

The Marxist challenge to uninvolved or compromised ecclesiastical institutions was not only in the meaning of love, but also in the realm of action and power. In his emphasis on deeds, not words, Marx reflected the same concern as the Apostle Paul: 'For the Kingdom of God is not in word, but in power.'

The pre-requisite of any revolution is power: the knowledge of where power lies, the way it is structured, and how it can be harnessed to accomplish the ends of the revolutionary individual or group. Marx analysed this central issue, Lenin compromised it, Stalin abused it, and Mao exploited it, but all were aware of it. Marx rejected any idealistic perspective which posed ideal ends without incorporating in this reflection the actual dynamic of a concrete reality. But he insisted that human action is characterised by the ability to plan purposeful action, to incorporate rational goals into everyday activity, and so he rejected all opportunistic action in which revolutionary intention was not in every aspect of strategy and tactics. 'If a man is shaped by circumstances,' said Marx, 'it follows that it is necessary to give them human form.'

Engels, in distinguishing between the philosophical conception of the state and the state as a power reality, said the former 'is the realisation of the idea, or the Kingdom of God on earth ... the sphere in which eternal justice is or should be realised', while the latter is 'nothing but a machine for the oppression of one class by another, in the democratic republic no less than in the monarchy.'

This Marxist emphasis on the realisation of the idea has been taken up by the Latin American Christians in their 'theology of liberation', and in the central emphasis on 'praxis'. The Brazilian Christian educator, Paulo Freire, has written: 'Liberation is a praxis: the action and reflection of men upon their world in order to transform it ... Within the world we find two dimensions, reflection and action, in such radical interaction that if one is sacrificed, even in part, the other immediately suffers ...'[12] Theologians such as Gustavo Gutierrez, Jose Miguez Bonino and Jose Miranda are representatives of this movement, finding parallels between Marxism and Christianity and using them with such dynamic and transforming effect in Latin America in the past ten years.

Fidel Castro is reported to have said, half-jokingly, that he felt confused because so many 'theologians are becoming communists and communists are becoming theologians'. In his book, *Christians and Marxists*, Jose Miguez Bonino writes:

> Juan Rosales, an Argentine Marxist author who has given careful attention — and much incisive criticism — to the role of religion in our society, makes this rather startling assertion:
> '...the bringing about of a true revolutionary transformation in our country... is for us (communists) *inconceivable* without the resolute participation of a renewed and engaged Christianity, which is equipped to make its specific contribution to the revolutionary baggage.'
> ...But right and left, ecclesiastical hierarchies and the common man in the street, the social analyst and the journalist, Latin Americans and foreign observers are equally arrested by this new phenomenon: not a Christian-Marxist dialogue but a growing and overt common participation in a revolutionary project, the basic lines of which are undoubtedly based on Marxist analysis...

Marxist Rituals

Revolution, the French writer Jean-Francois Revel has declared, 'is a total social fact', that is, it affects every facet of a culture. By definition, therefore, 'a revolutionary situation exists when, in every cultural area of a society, old values are in the process of being rejected, and new values have been prepared to replace them.'

Every human revolution has at least four things in common, whatever the thrust of the desire for change. One, an unsatisfactory, dying, or out-moded social, moral, political or other framework which the majority of people feel — some vaguely, some clearly — needs to be changed: two, a personality, or leader, whose clarity of perception enables him clearly to pin-point the precise things that are wrong, and whose creativity makes him the catalyst of necessary change: three, a band of initial followers, very often small in number, who see clearly what is wrong, and who see the rightness of the leader's analysis and proposed remedies: four, a body of writing which preserves the analysis and demonstrates clearly the remedies proposed so that the least educated of people can understand.

What distinguishes revolution from evolution, according to W.F. Wertheim, in his book *Evolution and Revolution*, is the cataclysmic character of the social change brought about. And Hannah Arendt has argued that there seems to be an additional quality in the concept of revolution which places it in a different category from 'revolt' or 'rebellion' or 'mutiny'. That difference seems to lie in the criterion that a revolution always aims at an overthrow of the existing social order and of the prevalent power structure, whereas all the other types of protest, whatever they may be called, simply aim to deal a selected blow at those in authority and lack this vital aspiration to fundamental change of existing society. Mao Tse-tung summed up Marxism by declaring: 'Marxism consists of a thousand truths but they all boil down to one sentence: It is right to rebel.'

Revolution, then, is the lifestyle of Marxist truth, and the many and varied activities of Marx's followers throughout the world in pursuit of this lifestyle have now become accepted rituals; strikes, boycotts, gathering of petitions, organising of private or public meetings, demonstrations, days of protest, barricading of streets, pamphleteering, campaigns on popular issues of discontent, refusal to pay taxes, picketing, kidnapping of political figures, sloganeer-ing.

All of these externalised Marxist rituals are directed towards the revolutionary change in society to be brought about by the inherent and inevitable consequences of sacramental economic doctrinal revelation boldly outlined in the *Manifesto* and detailed in *Capital*. Just as a sacrament is a religious ceremony or act regarded as the outward and visible signs of an inward and spiritual grace, so the now widely recognised Marxist externalised rituals — from the most jejune sloganeering, jeans and jargon to the most profound social analysis — are justified and sanctified by reference to the mysterious and sacred significance and influence of the 'laws' discovered by Marx. These necessary 'laws' can be scientifically determined by economic analysis; the laws are laws of a dynamic process, and so the direction of the process can be predicted: and just as it is the relationship of productive forces in any system which shapes the expression of that system, whether in morals, religion or political organisation, so the way in which 'history' has moved can be rationally understood; and the way in which it will move in the future can be scientifically predicted. Included are: revelation, redemption, salvation, assurance, death to self and new life in conversion experience, penance for sins committed, forgiveness when penance observed, and the promise of a future utopian communist kingdom.

Marxist Ethics

All political philosophies are moral as well as intellectual creations; they contain by their very nature high ideals, sophisticated theories, grand-sounding slogans, primitive propaganda and dubious facts. It is in challenging men and women to the high ideals that the necessity for ethics arises, an articulation of ideals which on various levels of generality and sophistication* is used in judging individuals, circum-

---

* It is interesting and amusing to note that even the dictionaries have problems in defining 'ethics', giving as its meaning 'morals and the regulation of conduct', while under 'morals' giving the meaning 'ethics and regulating of conduct'.

stances, and movements, and as goals and guidelines for aspirations, policies and an enthusiastic following. Thus the young Marx, as image-maker of a utopian communist future, sets out his ideals, his Ten Beatitudes:

    (i)   Expropriation of landed property, and the use of land rents to defray state expenditure.

   (ii)   A vigorously graduated income tax.

  (iii)   Abolition of the right of inheritance.

  (iv)   Confiscation of the property of all *emigrés* and rebels.

   (v)   Centralization of credit in the hands of the state, by means of a national bank with state capital and an exclusive monopoly.

  (vi)   Centralization of the means of transport in the hands of the state.

 (vii)   Increase of national factories and means of production, cultivation of uncultivated land, and improvement of cultivated land in accordance with a general plan.

(viii)   Universal and equal obligation to work; organization of industrial armies, especially for agriculture.

  (ix)   Agriculture and urban industry to work hand in hand, in such a way as by degrees to obliterate the distinction between town and country.

   (x)   Public and free education of all children. Abolition of factory work for children in its present form. Education and material production to be combined.

By means of these Ten Beatitudes all class distinctions would be swept away, all poverty abolished, all social, economic and political differences would be eliminated, all state apparatus and religious institutions would wither, and the kingdom of love and freedom would be ushered in.

Truth, honesty and integrity were declared as the essential prerequisites of communist party and communist individuals, both in Russia and in China. According to Lenin:

A political party's attitude to its own mistakes is one of the most important and sure ways of judging how earnest the party is and how it fulfils in practice its obligations to its class and the working people. Frankly acknowledging a mistake, analysing the conditions that have led up to it, and thrashing out the means of rectifying it — that is the hallmark of a serious party; that is how it should perform its duties; that is how it should educate and train its class and then its masses. From living perception to abstract thought, and from this to practice — such is the dialectical path of the cognition of truth, of the cognition of objective reality...

And Chairman Mao, in China, declared:

Our point of departure is to serve the people whole-heartedly and never for a moment divorce ourselves from the masses, to proceed in all cases from the interests of the people and not from the interests of individuals or groups, and to understand the identity of our responsibility to the people and our responsibility to the leading organs of the Party. Communists must be ready at all times to stand up for the truth, because truth is in the interests of the people; Communists must be ready at all times to correct their mistakes, because mistakes are against the interests of the people...

We must criticise and struggle with certain cadres and Party members, who have committed serious mistakes, and certain bad elements among the masses of workers and peasants. In such criticism and struggle we should persuade the masses to adopt correct forms and methods and to refrain from rough actions ... The other side is that these cadres, Party members and bad elements should be made to pledge that they will not retaliate against the masses. It should be announced that the masses not only have the right to criticise them freely but also have the right to dismiss them from their posts if necessary...

Thus Marxists set out to re-define the moral nature of people, and in place of worshipping God and obeying his commands they substituted idolising the masses and serving them. In the name of 'the masses' there emerged the new Marxist doctrines of standards of right and wrong, good and evil, in which society had to believe for its 'salvation'.

Marxism claimed that blueprints were not necessary, that it was sufficient to generalise and theoretically concentrate the rich experience of the workers themselves. Both Marx and Engels had learned from the Paris Commune that 'the dictatorship of the proletariat', workers' democracy, would mean the rule of the majority over the relics of the old exploiting minority. The state would thus not be a 'special apparatus of repression' but the direct rule of the working people. The masses would bear arms to defend their common property and power, and would participate in all administrative duties. From the first day of the revolution it would already only be a 'semi-state', which would wither away as the remnants of capitalism were overcome.

Workers' democracy was declared to be an organic form natural to any workers' organisations, from a shop stewards' committee, to a mass factory meeting, to any genuinely democratic centralist party, and, at the highest level, to Soviets — as organic as *'koinonia'* (fellowship) was to Christianity. There were said to be four fundamental safeguards against the 'place-hunting and other careerism' practised by Marxist non-believers:

  (i)   No official was to receive a wage higher than that of the average skilled worker.
  (ii)   Administrative duties were to be rotated among the widest strata of the working population, to prevent developing a bureaucratic caste.
  (iii) All working people were to bear arms, to safeguard the revolution against any threat, external or internal.
  (iv)   All power was to be vested in the Soviets.

Marxist Mythologies

But new myths had to be found to substantiate this new twentieth-century religion, and these emerged from the revolutionary struggle to implant bolshevism in Russia. The early Marxists had not considered Russia a suitable country for the new communism — they had assumed England and America as more likely targets — but once committed to the transformation of Russia the mythology had to be consolidated and perpetuated.

In the summer and autumn of 1917, the two most brilliant Russian revolutionaries, Lenin and Trotsky, came together to solidify bolshevism, and it was their different doctrines taken together which coincided to make up bolshevism as theory, strategy and ideology. This was the crucial event in the Marxist myth — the fact of the Russian revolution, the way in which it occurred, where it occurred, how it grew and was consolidated, the leaders who had to become mythic figures to sustain the new religion. But the Marxist 'Trinity' of Marx, Lenin and Stalin, which the Russians worked so hard to have accepted, will be replaced by history with Marx, Lenin and Mao — father, son and holy spirit.

However, the victory of the bolsheviks such as Lenin and Trotsky over the social democrats such as Klautsky and Rosa Luxemburg showed the gaps in Marx's thinking, and opened the way for controversies and heresies. Socialist democracy was about how to install socialism in advanced capitalist nations with parliamentary systems. Bolshevism was about how to make a revolution in an economically backward country having a despotic government. The importance of this distinction is that Marxists have never been able to reconcile the various socialist aims with Marx's theories, and so myths have had to be produced about people and policies. For in the century since Marx in no advanced capitalist society has a revolution of proletarian or bolshevik type succeeded; bolshevik revolutions, in the name of Marx, have succeeded only in backward peasant societies with autocratic governments. This has been noted — and admitted — by leading Russian communists, such as, for example, Fyodor V. Konstantinov, the editor-in-chief of *Kommunist*, the leading theoretical organ of the Communist Party of the Soviet Union[13] (Footnote: See *The Marxists*, Penguin Books, C. Wright Mills, p. 451).

But the variety of interpretations of the Master's doctrines has given rise to an Apostolate that is recognised by one or other streams of Marxism being believed and practised in a number of countries. The 'Twelve Apostles' of Marx responsible for developing and communicating in one form or another the Marxist mythology were:

Friedrich Engels, closest colleague of Marx in most important ideas and writings, whose distinctive contribution was to warn against employing concepts and ideas as a substitute for the concrete study of real historical facts.

Eduard Bernstein, German Social Democrat who became the chief champion of 'revisionism' and 'reformism', i.e., of *revising* Marx's theories so as to demonstrate that a socialist revolution was unnecessary, that the workers could get all they wanted by reforms.

Karl Kautsky, leading Marxist theoretician in the Second International, a Darwinist who applied the concepts of heredity and adaptability to the environment to his views on the law of social development.

M.A. Bakunin, Russian anarchist friend and early colleague of Marx in the First International, which Marx broke up rather than compromise with Bakunin.

Rosa Luxemburg, one of the greatest leaders of the German Social Democratic Party and co-founder of the German Communist Party. She emphasised social development and the idea that an economic crisis would probably be the starting point for the proletariat seizing power as their development conformed with certain laws.

George V. Plekhanov, the leading Russian Marxist before Lenin, who founded the first group of Russian Marxists, but was a 'menshevik' and not a 'bolshevik' and so was superseded.

V.I. Lenin, embodied the Marxist ideal of 'the unity of theory and practice' and developed the theory of permanent revolution under the leadership of the proletariat; also emphasised the basic idea of historical materialism that 'out of one form of social life, as the result of the growth of productive forces, another higher form develops.'

Leon Trotsky, grasped the idea of permanent revolution and attempted in the name of traditional Marxist ideas to fight against the swing to 'constructive socialism' in Russia, against its construction in one single country: these conflicts, he argued, could only be resolved on an international scale in the arena of a world-wide proletarian revolution.

G. Zinoviev, argued that the immediate task was to make communism work in Russia, and that the regime was then strong enough to attack the *kulaks* (village capitalists).

N.I. Bukharin, opposed both Stalin and Trotsky on a number of issues, including failure to understand the nature of the Russian revolution.

Joseph Stalin, opposed Trotsky's 'extreme intellectualism' and expelled him and many others from the Party: he closely unified the theory and practice of Marxism, while brutally segregating them to suit himself without scruple; all to consolidate and industrialize the Soviet State at any price, including political tyranny and police coercion.

Antonio Gramsci, Italian Marxist who, in contrast to Plekhanov's interpretation, called historical laws 'laws of tendency' and said that they should not be interpreted in the same sense as the laws of natural history or in the spirit of a speculative determinism.

These are the leading Marxist mythic figures whose development or modification of Marx's original writings have become institutionalised in one form or another in twentieth century international Marxist doctrine. With Lenin's death in 1924, Trotsky's exile in 1929, and the failure to produce another similar successful revolution in Western Europe, the original bolshevism and much of the original ethos of Leninism ended, and Stalinism completed the erosion of the early Marxism. This was the period of 'socialist construction', of forced industrialisation and collectivisation — as destructive to classical Marxist ideals as Constantine's institutionalising of the Church was to those of Christ's — when Russia grew into a powerful industrial state in the short period of one generation and became, in the words of several disillusioned Communists, 'the god that failed'.

It was in the area of *human* failings, though, that Marx's communism in Russia and Eastern Europe failed. Greed for power, greed for money, greed for comfort, greed for national expansion, greed for personal and national status, were all indulged with a merciless and unprincipled brutality by Stalin and fellow-communists in the name of Marx, and in a modified form in other countries.

Of the seven original 'Politburo' members in October 1917, Lenin died, Zinoviev and Kamenov were executed, Sokolnikov was in prison, Bubnov had 'disappeared', and Trotsky was in exile in March 1938. By March 1938, of the twenty-four members of the Central Committee of the Party in 1917, seven had died natural deaths, six had been executed, six had 'disappeared', one had committed suicide, one was in prison, and one was 'retired'. Of both groups, only Stalin remained.

There is no longer any such thing as 'Marxism'. The work of Marx and Engels, which gave birth to the genetic term, has been used indiscriminately as the goad of liberalism, of social democracy, of bolshevism and Stalinism, as well as of capitalism. The institutionalised streams of selective communist ideology that have sprung from the founder's writings are as diverse and often as distant from their source as the many forms of other institutionalised religions.

Classical Marxism of the high ideal of a just and moral society failed because the followers of Marx betrayed those ideals in their neglect of the spiritual nature of man, and their calculated emphasis on man as only a social and economic animal. In his admirable book, *A Christian Commentary on Communism*,[14] Edward Rogers has summed up the dilemma facing Marxism in the twentieth century, as it faced Marx himself in the nineteenth century;

> The problems posed by Communism are ultimately religious. The practical problems are moral, the theoretical problems are theological, and the factor which cannot be ignored without disaster is sin.

2

Communism and Christianity

ALAN SCARFE

The Christian Church has faced no greater challenge in its
checkered history than that of communism. Communists not
only rub off the face-lifting cosmetics of a so-called Christian
society by pointing the finger of mocking justice at the real
face of christianised capitalism, but they offer in turn to build
a completely new order of humanity. They bring to a
mankind weary of half-hearted reforms and mass indiffer-
ence a fresh vision of total change which promises to leave
nothing of the old order intact and which they set out to create
in apparently manageable proportions; clear steps to transformation in an increasingly confusing and unwieldy world.

This combination of uncompromising analysis and dis-
tinguishable programme is its main attraction, and the
Church faces the consequence of its own failure to provide
anything of equal proportions, preferring on the whole to sit
on privilege rather than service for others. Communists judge
the Church by history and they affirm that their own faith —
for their political and economic dogma can be likened to
articles of faith — can and will produce better results in one
twentieth of the time.

The scope of this paper is to assess the Christian reaction to
communism in the light of basic communist attitudes towards Christianity. There are Christians in Latin America

and the Third World who see in communism a way of social revolution which will not only liberate the working peoples of the world but also regain for the Church her true perspective as the Servant Church, seeking to carry out in physical terms the 'Nazareth Manifesto' of Luke 4. These Christians contrast with those within existing socialist states who by force of circumstances have had to develop a similar theology. The problem for Latin American Christians is whether to participate in the violence of the revolution. For the East Europeans it is often how to keep silent about the post-revolutionary violence. The dilemma of the latter neutralises the impact of the former in the eyes of the majority of the uncommitted. The Latin American situation will be discussed in another article. The purpose of this article is to look at the basic doctrinal positions of communism regarding Christianity.

Communism, it must be said, is a many-sided creature. No so-called communist state would say that it has achieved communism. Communism is rather the eternal state of continuous development which all 'communist' regimes are aiming for. At the present time they would classify themselves as 'socialist'. In the socialist stage the Communist Party, its members still a minority in society, establishes the rule for the proletariat, the masses of the working force, until society is reordered and the new principles of Marxism-Leninism are fully functional in the economic, social and 'spiritual' life of the country. Eventually the state structure can be abolished, it will wither away, and the new communist society with no leaders, no superstructure, no bureaucracy will emerge. Work will be controlled by workers' committees; censorship will be abolished and each journalistic enterprise will discern the propriety of its material for itself. Wrong-doers will be dealt with within society, being corrected without the necessity of prison. Money too will be done away with and people will work to the best of their ability for the good of all, receiving material goods in accordance with their needs. Ultimately the system will extend to the whole world.

Such is the theory, and to fulfil it man himself must be changed. The new socialist man is to be produced from among the generation of youth educated aright under the socialist system. The youth will embody the principles of Marxism-Leninism taught at school, university and on the factory floor, and will be ready selflessly to put communism into practice.

It is the interpretation of how these basic doctrines are to be implemented, how the transformation is to take place, which causes the confusion. Eurocommunism, for example, seeks to work its way forward by influencing the political systems already existing in Western Europe, leading them to a gradual change. Its adherents are acutely conscious of the bad impression created by the barbarism of their counterparts in the Soviet Union and in Eastern Europe. They promise transformation without denying human rights and without resorting to violence. In contrast, Asian and Latin American Communist Parties see no alternative to violent revolution to accomplish their objectives. In Asia it is further believed that revolution does not stop at the achieving of political power. There must be a continual struggle within the country. No opportunity must be given for a new elite to establish a privileged ruling class. This is what the Chinese criticise in the Soviet Union. There, and in Eastern Europe, the ongoing revolution is discriminate. After the revolution which set the Party in power the system has solidified, causing repression for those of both Marxist or non-Marxist persuasion who are critical of the government in any way. Stability and security are considered the required ingredients for progress towards communism. Thus, for example, negative descriptions of society in the media are to be discouraged as reducing morale.

These three attitudes or interpretations stem from the same basic thoughts of Marx, Engels and Lenin. The writings of these three constitute the "Scriptures of Communism". Their commentators, Trotsky, Stalin, Mao and the modern equivalents, represent varied methods for putting theory into practice. It is important, therefore, when we consider the reaction of Christianity to communism that we know the correct standpoint of the particular form of communism being presented to us. Our response should be equally particular.

So just as we cannot assume a monolithic character in

communism, even in Europe, neither can we expect a blanket attitude on the part of the communist states towards religion. There are distinct differences in the treatment of religious groups in Eastern Europe and in the Soviet Union. It is these attitudes we will now discuss. In doing so, however, further definitions need to be made.

Not all that one sees portrayed as flagrant communist opposition to religion can justly be put down to ideological conviction. Non-ideological factors determine some of the antagonism and also some of the differences of approach towards religion in the various communist countries. The first factor to consider is nationalism. For example, the nationalist feelings of the people of Poland and their historical identity with the Roman Catholic Church to a large extent protect the Church from attack despite its criticism of the government. The government, already unsure of its popularity with its own people, could not risk the effects of a purge of outstanding Church leaders. A similar situation exists in Romania with the Orthodox Church, but there the lie of good relations between church and state is exposed by the presence of substantial minority groups of non-Orthodox character who do not enjoy the state's toleration to the same extent. In the Soviet Union the nationalist question works against the churches. In Ukraine and Lithuania the Catholic communities suffer acute persecution. Those imprisoned or banned from practising their faith openly are often persecuted on the grounds of their alleged 'anti-sovietism' and 'retrograde nationalist tendencies'. Nevertheless at the same time the national identity of Church with people keeps the faithful close to the Church.

The second major factor of non-ideological character which may determine the religious policy of a communist government is the international climate. The communist parties have found themselves still in need of capitalism to bolster their own economic systems. Trade contacts are therefore important. Prestige, too, on the international stage goes hand in hand with the world-wide purposes of communism. It is good propaganda to be seen to enhance individual freedom. Hence alongside trade agreements go cultural exchanges and representation in international organisations, including religious bodies. The Church can thereby become a useful messenger of good tidings for the socialist state. On the other hand it can also become an embarrassment, for increased international relations has also opened up the way for human rights activitists of both a secular and a religious nature. They have understood the possibilities before them and by their brave appeals have helped us to understand them too. Their presence within state-recognised religious bodies which play the diplomatic role have caused and still do cause considerable problems for the government: their approach to religion must therefore take this into consideration too.

We ought now to turn to the ideological factors, the communist 'Scriptures'. Marx had no doubt about the role of religion in the capitalist order. It was so much a creation of capitalism that it would disappear with the disappearance of capitalism. Engels saw in early Christianity a primitive form of communism, but without the further development of the historical process from which communism would inevitably arise the Christian experiment had no hope of becoming anything more than a brief portent of the future. Christianity was doomed to become the outward expression of the economic systems which encompassed it, bolstering up and justifying the exploitation of feudalism (answered in Christian terms by Catholicism) and capitalism (and Protestantism its religious expression).

Christianity became part of the ruling philosophy of each age. It did more than justify the sins of the exploiters. Marx admitted that it served a purpose for the workers too. Religion soothed the pains and hardships of the present by offering them the assurance of happiness in the after-life. They adhered to Christianity for hope and comfort and also as a means of expressing their oppressed feelings. On their part the oppressors were able to ease their consciences through religion. They justified the class system by Scripture. As Lenin wrote, commenting on Marx, in *Socialism and Religion:*

Those who toil and live in want all their lives are taught by religion to be submissive and patient whilst on earth and to take comfort in the hope of the heavenly reward. But those who live by the labour of others are taught by religion to practise charity

while on earth, thus offering them a cheap way of justifying their
entire existence as exploiters and selling them at a moderate price
tickets to well-being in heaven. Religion is the opium for the
people.

Thus it was thought that religion would be rendered
redundant and outmoded once communism was achieved,
for the political, social and economic order in which it was
rooted would have been destroyed. The real world would be
able to proceed with the task of fulfilling human aspirations
without having to resort to any excuse about resting or
waiting upon the "gods". All those charlatans and indi-
vidualists who had been earning their non-productive living
off the backs of the people's 'expression of distress' would be
done away with too.

Religion, however, was not only an economic aid; it also
reflected something of man's psychological condition. The
capitalist order had estranged man from himself. The oppressive economic system and especially its valuation of human
beings according to their productivity had caused man to lose
his own sense of worth and the worth of his own creativity.
Thus estranged man projected the subsequent sense of
non-fulfilment into the realm of the mystical, enjoying
spiritual fulfilment in worshipping the 'gods':

> Man's alienation from things is the practice of his alienation from
> himself. Thus man, as long as he remains a prisoner to religion,
> does not know how to objectify his being except by making of it a
> foreign fantastic being; similarly under the domination of this
> egotistical necessity he cannot act directly, or produce directly,
> except by putting his products and his activity under the
> domination of a foreign element: money. Karl Marx: *Jewish
> Problem*.

Religion as the reflection of man's oppression needed to be
replaced by true happiness and prosperity, by the restoration
of that state of things whereby he was once more united with
himself, his creativity and his society. This could only be
achieved through the destruction of capitalism:

> The distress of religion is the expression of the real distress and is
> at the same time the protest against that distress: religion is the

sign of the oppressed creature, the sensibility of a world devoid of heart, it is the spirit of an order devoid of spirit. It is opium for the people. Suppression of this illusory happiness is the requirement of true happiness. To renounce the illusion with regard to oneself is to renounce the situation which gives rise to the need for the illusion. The criticism of religion is therefore the criticism of this wave of weeping whose aroma is religion. Marx: *Critique of Hegelian Philosophy of Law.*

Marx saw little benefit in attacking religion, since he expected it to wither away in the changed circumstances. In fact he warned of the danger of creating religious martyrs. His theories of the role of religion, however, were never put into practice in his lifetime. But soon after the October Revolution in 1917 the Russian Orthodox Church began to feel the effects. The inevitable disappearance of religion was not easy to bring about and Lenin, Stalin, Khruschev and Brezhnev have since all found themselves more than occupied with assisting the inevitability along its way. The grounds for repressing religious believers were provided for in Marx's teaching. Christianity, and especially the Orthodox Church under the Czar, being defined as an integral part of the capitalist system obviously contained members of a reactionary character who would continue to use the religious consolation to keep people opposed to the new socialist order. Capitalists of old would seek to hide behind the cassocks of the priests in their endeavour to hold on to what they could of the past. To persecute such a Church was not considered an attack on religion (religion was not *that* important) but rather an attack on the image of religion used as a cover for anti-socialist politics.

Changing the habits of the religious populace was another problem. There was need for re-education in order that the new generation of socialists could be raised to put things quickly into order. Re-education was needed too in the realm of religion. In *Socialism and Religion* Lenin said:

Our programme is based entirely on the scientific and materialistic world outlook. An explanation of our programme, therefore, necessarily includes an explanation of the true and historical roots of the religious fog. Our propaganda necessarily includes the propaganda of atheism.

The Party's task was therefore simple — to expose the sins of the Church in allowing itself to be used by those hiding their anti-socialist sympathies behind the religious mask, and to expose the unscientific inadequacies of the religious life view through atheist teaching. In connection with the former, mock trials were held to denounce church dignatories as scandalous renegades.

Lenin placed great hope in the re-education programme. Atheist teaching was not just the straight-forward denial of the existence of God and the explanation of the roots of religion, but included the positive philosophy of scientific atheism and the creation of the new socialist man, which was an urgent matter. It became clear to Lenin that external changes were not sufficient to create the new order. Individual transformation through education was essential. Furthermore the persistent attraction of religion demanded more than mock trials and deterrents of that nature. Lenin therefore examined the psychological implication of Marx's theory of alienation. He called for a re-examination of man's centre of motivation.

Like Marx, he concluded that man's interest in religion stemmed from his estrangement from nature. Through his relationship with nature man searched out the knowledge of all things. In dominating nature for profit and in becoming himself dominated by capital, man's search for knowledge through his examination of nature was lost. He thus projected his search into the realms of the mystical. God became the source of all knowledge. A return to the scientific concept of the world would set man back on course to understand things correctly. True knowledge and a true understanding of nature would both be opened up to man through scientific materialism. To continue in enchantment with mystical ideas was evidence of a retrograde mentality. In certain cases this was stretched to declaring believers insane because of their belief. The pilgrim had stopped along the Pilgrim's Way to the Palace of Scientific Materialism and Technology. The classification of believers as mentally retarded creatures, even perhaps as clinically insane, is a direct result of Lenin's search for human motivation, based on Marx. Human motivation is still being discussed by Marxists in the Western world but a different assessment of Christianity is reached in their analysis. This is dealt with elsewhere.

Marx in *Capital* wrote:

> Religious reflections of the real world can in any case only then vanish when practical relations of everyday life offer to man none but perfectly intelligible and reasonable relations with regard to his fellowmen and nature.

Sixty years later religion in the Soviet Union is as vibrant and relevant to millions as ever, and the state's concern with it continues to be intense: but neither atheist teaching, though increased and refined, nor direct repression has succeeded in stemming the constant flood of new converts to every denomination. The same can be seen throughout Eastern Europe. Yet broadly speaking the traditional communist treatment of religion remains the same. The capitalist tendencies of the Church are repeatedly 'proven' in the eyes of the socialist authorities by its links with Western church organisations, especially the missions. They ignore the fact that the severe curtailing of the publication possibilities of the Church has made it look for assistance from outside. Religion therefore constitutes a thorny dilemma for the Communist Party today, for its continued presence demonstrates the contradictions within the Marxist-Leninist position. This would be so even without the added contemporary problem of the human rights activists, amongst whom Christians are prominent, though not as numerous as is generally believed.

Lenin spelled out the dilemma from the outset:

> We ask that religion be considered a private question in reference to the state, but in no way can it be considered a private matter as far as the Party is concerned... Everyone must have the full right to profess any religion, or not to recognise religion, that is, to be an atheist, as every socialist should normally be. But it is inadmissable to make any distinction between citizens on the grounds of their rights to practise their religious faith. *Socialism and Religion*.

In a state where responsibility for education, government, social and industrial development has been assumed by the

Communist Party Lenin's distinction failed to mean anything but an unworkable constitutional right. That right was
further limited in subsequent constitutions. The Party's good
intentions to grant democratic freedom have continued to
clash with its intentions to create a socialist democracy, and
religion has suffered in the conflict.

Some might claim that in recent years there has, however,
been a significant reappraisal of religion within the socialist
state. The purges of Stalin and Khruschev which decimated
the Church have ceased. The major denominations of Eastern
Europe participate in the world bodies of the Christian
Church, e.g. the World Council of Churches and the Baptist
World Alliance. But what we see here is only a variation on
the old Marxist-Leninist theme. This variation is more easily
perceptible in the countries of Eastern Europe than in the
Soviet Union, though it is true of both areas: what you cannot
remove by force from without, first accommodate, then
manipulate. Within this theory of accommodation, however,
there is in some countries a patriotic appreciation by the
socialist governments of the historical and cultural role of the
Church in the past, as well as a belief in its diplomatic
usefulness for the present and part of the future. Yet in
conceding some freedoms to the Church the Party is permit-
ting an ideological alternative to continue in its midst which
may from time to time prove to be a critical embarrassment to
its own ideological ends: Poland is a case in point.

In the Orthodox world the Romanian Church has been
likened to the Polish Catholic Church in its strength and
relations with the state. Indeed there is a special relationship
between the Orthodox Church of Romania and the Romanian
Communist Party. In an interview given in the Congo in 1974
the President of Romania, Nicolae Ceausescu, said that
religion was a phenomenon which could be expected to
survive for a long time yet. The socialist state had to accept the
presence of the churches in its society, whilst not compromis-
ing upon its own scientific materialist concept of life and the
world. The same thoughts were reiterated back home by
Ceausescu in the United Socialist Front Congress on 24 May
1974, where the denominations were represented for the first
time. In welcoming the representatives of the fourteen legally

recognised denominations in Romania to the United Socialist Front Congress, President Ceausescu publicly recognised that the Church was clearly a significant force in maintaining unity and peace within society. Unity of the Romanian people could only be achieved, said Ceausescu, by co-operation between all forces within society, including the religious forces:

> In speaking of the realization of the complete unity of the entire people around the Party, I consider it essential that we define, within this framework, the place of religion and the religious denominations in our society.
>
> We start out convinced of the necessity to respect the human conscience and that includes the religious beliefs of every citizen in the land. Of course as communists we promote the historical, Marxist-dialectical concepts of life and the world, and we base our actions on and around these scientific concepts. Yet at the same time we have respected and continue to respect the convictions of others, especially religious beliefs and their right to be practised. In fact it is well known that clear provision is made in the Constitution of the country to ensure the normal functioning of the denominations' activity and the practice of religion. In conformity with these provisions fourteen religious denominations whose status is recognised by the state are active today in Romania. On these grounds the denominations have their well defined place in the state.

Repeating how essential that place was in helping to fulfil the socialist goals of society, Ceausescu added a note of warning which is strikingly familiar:

> Although faith is a personal matter of conscience for each citizen... we must at the same openly state that all citizens, regardless of their philosophical convictions or religious beliefs, must respect the laws of the land with devotion.

Unfortunately in this context the laws of the land do not simply protect society from crime and violence, but they are also used to dictate the direction of society towards the goals of socialism, towards the achievement of communism. For example, the ideological attitude of teachers, doctors, lawyers and other professionals became legislative matter in Romania

in 1975 when the swearing of an oath of allegiance to the
internal policies of the Party, including its atheist teaching,
was required of all in these professions. Those who refused to
swear the oath on grounds of conscience lost their jobs or
were demoted. Thus, 'devotion to the law' may in certain
circumstances be too exclusive a commitment for the
Christian. A more costly and familiar illustration of this is the
position of the Reformed Baptists in the Soviet Union. They
rejected the state's requirements for registration as a legally
recognised denomination in 1961. And in rejecting official
legal recognition they found themselves outside the protec-
tion of the law, with the subsequent risk of the imprisonment
of their leaders, fining of their meetings and removal of the
meeting houses.

Nevertheless, Ceausescu's words at the United Socialist
Front Congress and the evidence of a materially flourishing
Church in Romania give reason for hope that a new religious
policy is being worked out. Contradictions within the Party's
position still remain, however, for though the modern
socialist state encourages religious exchanges and participation in international conferences at home as well as abroad
and, in general, wants the Church to be seen to be playing an
active part within the socialist democracy, individual
Christians of legally recognised denominations, as well as those
like the Reformed Baptists, are often suffering discrimination in
their domestic situation, sometimes during the very course of
such international conferences. The events in the Soviet Union
during the Belgrade review conference of the Helsinki
Agreement in 1977/78 reflect this, where 18 individuals were
gradually rounded up for attempting to monitor their country's
record on keeping the Helsinki Agreement!

The policy of accommodation aims to wed the Church to
the pleasant aspects of the Party's national policy and, if
possible, to get the Church to voice its ideological slogans,
though using theological or 'spiritual' language. No criticism
of society is allowed, nor can society benefit from the
Church's alternative viewpoint on matters of Party internal
policies. Peace, social justice (interpreted in Marxist terms)
and anti-colonialism are the messages from the pulpits in
many places, and even where the Gospel is soundly preached

it is often without any practical application. But this subtle process of stripping the Church of its spiritual treasures has not fooled the general populace of the faithful. They search out the preaching of those who have refused to bow down to the secularisation of the Church in this way. The state's policy fails to prevent the growth of the Church and, more danger-ously for them, creates popular cult figures within the Church whose spiritual authority is acknowledged because of their uncompromising and fearless preaching. The policy also gives rise to smaller, uncontrollable groups meeting in private to supplement their spiritual diet.

However, accommodation at least means that in spite of the tensions the doors are open between the Church and the state both internally and externally. In view of the increased highlighting of human rights issues and the trade co-operation between Western and Eastern Europe, state accom-modation would seem to be the prevalent policy for the future. The same will be true as long as the balance of power in Western governments tips favourably towards the Marxists. International prestige must be kept at a high level whilst comrades woo voters. It would be folly for them to ignore the influence of the Church in the Western societies.

Alongside the process of accommodation there lies a more aggressive development, that of substitution. This is the root of the Party's hostility towards religion. The destruction of religion alone is not the Party's aim, but rather the creation of a new system of personal and social behaviour of a humanist nature and motivation. They seek to create a new man for the new socialist society. Without him they cannot build com-munism, and religion must therefore be replaced by a non-religious framework of values and convictions. It would not be sufficient for the Party simply to employ the successful Western methods of commercial materialism and good enter-tainments to reduce the impact of religion! Good television programmes on a Sunday evening would not be their answer for their aims are higher. It is true, however, that alternative activities for the young are often arranged on Sundays, such as outings with the Young Communist organisations on Sunday mornings, or compulsory patriotic work; and that special competitions which count towards future job and career prospects are also arranged to counter the attraction of church-going. But all this is done for the purpose of utilising leisure time for the creation of the new man. Religion is discouraged because it hinders that process. Even where the Church is willing to work together with the Party on the humane aspects of its programme, the end product is inevitable substitution. As a Soviet ideologist recently reminded his comrades:

> Thus the involvement of believers in the struggle for communism does not conceive of any ideological compromise between Marxism and religion. Moreover, the participation of believers in the struggle for the transformation of society on a communist basis speeds up their acceptance of the scientific materialistic outlook. ...Thus to strengthen and broaden the unity of workpeople in the struggle for communism, to propagate successfully the scientific materialistic world outlook and thus quicken the pace of the withering away of religion, it is imperative to apply Lenin's principles on religion in their entirety.

The new man needs no God to lean on. He will base his life on the scientific materialistic world outlook. The new man has been described thus:

> The Party has sought to fashion a new political culture and to rear a new Soviet man, whose noble character traits and behaviour will be worthy of the ultimate communist society. In place of individualism, bourgeois nationalism, chauvinism, indolence and religious prejudices, there will be intelligent, creative and human citizens, imbued with feelings for collectivism, proletarian internationalism, social patriotism, love of labour and militant atheism.

In 1971 Ceausescu, impressed by the Cultural Revolution in China, initiated a citizenship programme to hasten the emergence of the new man. He launched a thirty-point ethical code to formulate the behaviour of the new man. Christian ethics were a thing of the past. The bold scheme, however, with its idealistic goals appears to have floundered.

Some communists, mainly in the West, have become very aware of the failure of the Soviets and East Europeans to motivate their people. The Czech philosopher, Vladislav Gadavsky, though asserting the essential atheist character of communism, asked communists to look more appreciatively at the achievements of Christianity in this respect. The Christian concept of love was for him the attraction. Communism needed to emphasise love as the motivating force for the new society, and Christ had much to teach on this subject both in words and also his own example. Gadavsky was nevertheless unbending in his conviction of the centrality of atheism within the communist ideological system. His participation in dialogue with Christians came to an end with the Soviet invasion of Czechoslovakia in 1968. Gadavsky was removed from his post in the University of Brno — an ironical end to a philosophical adventure which sought to harness the concept of Christian love and the higher aims of communism.

The Czechoslovakian invasion also injured, but not irreparably, other attempts between Christians and communists to come together. French communist Roger Garaudy was the chief proponent of dialogue before his resignation from the French Communist Party in 1968. He still calls for the development of a Christian Marxism, which for him constitutes the only viable alternative for the future of mankind. He urged his colleagues to see in Christianity the two essentials lacking in the socialist systems of the Soviet Union and Eastern Europe: the dynamism of faith and the motivation of love. He did not think atheism an essential part of the basic aims of the Party. In Christianity communism had an ally in overcoming the spiritual inadequacy of Marxism-Leninism. His form of revisionism was not widely applauded. It seems too, in probing deeper, that Garaudy's appeal for a coming together of Christianity and communism still resulted in an accentuation of the commandment to love man as oneself while ignoring the commandment to love God first. Garaudy accepted that to meet in dialogue there would need to be a compromise on both sides.

Christians within socialist regimes have been willing to offer their help in the impasse. They too single out atheism as the major bogey. It could, however, be argued that the whole ideological framework would be at stake. Granting freedom to Christians to contribute to the resolution of the contradictions within socialism might open the floodgates to ideas which could result in the loss of the Party's political monopoly and ultimately the communists' loss of power. Preserving the position of power is probably the major factor determining the state's attitude to Christianity. Hence one can view their moments of 'tolerance' as strategic expediencies. Nevertheless, there are Christians ready to offer their contribution to improve society, particularly in motivating the masses to build up the new society. Such Christians, however, ask to be allowed to contribute on their own terms without having to play along with socialist dogma in 'ecclesiastical language'. They claim that their contribution is valid only as the Gospel is free to be preached everywhere in society, without any accusations of 'retrograde mentality' or 'anti-scientific' behaviour, and only as God is acknowledged as more than an abstract optional extra for the unenlightened rather as the Being and Purpose of all things;

> Why is it that the new man refuses to appear in conformity to all the visions and expectations?... The present impasse, from a historical point of view, has been caused by the materialistic concept of man. The general materialistic world outlook is the very fact which maintains and will perpetuate the situation in which no example of the new man as a mass phenomenon will be able to appear...
>
> Materialism has created an immense spiritual vacuum. As long as the scientific world was shielded by a conviction of absolute knowledge, the emptiness was not felt. The emptiness was felt in moments of tragedy when science could no longer give a confident answer. Man's soul can never be satisfied with purely material and cultural goods. Man's soul thirsts for a spiritual world and cannot be satisfied with less than a living contact with it. Spiritual hunger, aspirations after the transcendent and an avid seeking of religious experience is the new dominant characteristic of the younger generation in the West and in the East, both in capitalist and socialist societies.
>
> Socialism needs the new man, the moral man, as man himself needs the air he breathes. This new man cannot be created by slogans or by moral codes of behaviour. Laws will never assist a man to become a moral being... Only the spirit of Christ can revolutionize a man, transform him and make him a new kind of

person. Socialism needs the spirit of Christ if it is to produce the new man. *Christian Manifesto*.

These words of challenge by Romanian Baptist Josif Ton offered in November 1974 have been expressed in different ways by numerous Christians to the various socialist governments in recent years. The proposal is not unique nor is it modern. Tertullian's argument to the Roman persecutors of the early Church ran along similar lines.

Christians in socialist societies affirm that they not only seek to live in peace for their sakes. (They are willing to pay the price of suffering for Christ's sake and all too often they have to.) But more importantly they claim that without them the whole of their society suffers. Man's greatest ally is found not in comrades or brothers who simply believe in the same things, thus giving one security, but in God who in Christ reconciled the world to himself, and thus potentially men to each other. An encounter with him brings a united strength out of diversity.

3

Sixty Years On
Reflection on the Practical Relations Between Christianity and Marxism-Leninism in the Soviet Union

KATHLEEN CARTER

Sixty years ago Lenin and his bolshevik party took control of the Russian state. Weakened by war and internal strife, it fell into their hands like an over-ripe apple. There followed years of civil war and famine that further devastated the country, but the bolsheviks held on. As they consolidated their control over the Russian nation, at the same time extending that rule to surrounding nationalities along the lines of the old Russian Empire, the bolsheviks gradually imposed their communist ideology upon ever wider areas of national life. This ideology included a militant atheism which, although toned down for the sake of specific objectives such as the inclusion of the Muslim areas of Central Asia, never departed from the Party's basic programme.

Since 1917, the pattern has not greatly changed. The Soviet Union has passed through terrible times of war, dictatorship and purges, and emerged as a highly-industrialised super-power, but the ideology remains. Over the years the atheist programme has from time to time and from region to region been soft-pedalled for specific and limited objectives, but it has never been fully set aside. This chapter looks at ways in which the official Soviet hostility to religion affects believers at different points of their life. It is not an exhaustive study, but every incident cited can be documented, and represents a piece of the complex jigsaw that is religious life in the USSR today.

'Religion is a fantastic, distorted reflection of the world in a man's consciousness,' says a Soviet textbook (*Sociology*, Moscow, 1969). Lenin regarded religion as a malady, a spiritual infection, a drug for the oppressed. These concepts have been accurately written into Soviet law. 'In order to ensure to citizens freedom of conscience, the church in the USSR is separated from the state, and the school from the church,' says the Soviet Constitution, Article 124. Despite the preamble, this means in practice that believers are cut off from every possible avenue of social influence, while the state reserves to itself maximum control over their every movement. This imbalance is actually given away in the second half of the same constitutional article, which states that 'freedom of religious worship and freedom of anti-religious propaganda are recognised for all citizens'. The fact is that the first Soviet Constitution, proclaimed in July 1918, included these words: 'the right to religious and anti-religious propaganda is recognised for all citizens'. In April 1929 Stalin passed the oppressive 'Law on Religious Associations' which, with a few alterations, is still in force today. A month later the relevant article of the Constitution was emended to sit more easily to the new law, and the words 'the right of religious profession' substituted for 'the right to religious propaganda'. The present wording represents an even narrower interpretation: implied in the words 'freedom of religious worship' is the right of believers to assemble together in certain buildings for strictly limited activities — nothing more.

For this purpose a limited number of 'special premises' are permitted to exist, where believers may 'satisfy their religious needs' (see the 1929 Law, paragraph 10). This last phrase is standard Soviet terminology. It has apparently become so much a part of people's thinking that even some believers themselves quote it in their appeals for greater religious liberty. But the use of these words exposes the total failure of Marxism-Leninism to understand the Christian faith. It is this misunderstanding which has led to the sometimes grotesque persecution of religion in the USSR.

It is within such 'special premises', and nowhere else, that regular religious services may take place. In this way, individuals who have already been infected with religion are to be isolated from society. At the same time, 'individual work' is carried on with the unfortunates to restore them to spiritual health, to a 'scientific' and materialist way of thinking. Atheist propaganda is also carried on with more or less persistency in the media and elsewhere, to maintain and strengthen ideological purity in the populace at large.

Despite all these measures, it is becoming increasingly evident that the religious epidemic is spreading in many areas. More and more intellectuals and Jews are turning to the Russian Orthodox Church for answers to their philosophical and cultural questions, and many are being baptised. The evangelical churches are seeing considerable growth. The Lithuanian Catholic Church offers a unique example of national and religious solidarity. Although some of this religious revival may amount to no more than a cultural swing, it is certain that in the midst of it all many genuine conversions are taking place.

Growing Up

For the Soviet Christian, the conflict between faith and environment penetrates every area of life. A young child is of course particularly vulnerable to outside influences. The fact that in the Soviet Union most mothers work, and many pre-school children attend a regular kindergarten, facilitates atheist influence from the earliest years of a child's life. Tension between a Christian home background and a non-Christian or anti-Christian school environment is not unique to the Soviet Union or other socialist states — it is beginning to be recognised as a serious problem even in this country. But Britain does not so far have the broadly-based legal framework for educational discrimination such as now exists in the Soviet Union.

Paragraph 17(c) of the 1929 Law forbids religious groups to 'organise special prayer or other meetings for children, young people and women, or general Bible, literary, handicraft, work, catechetical and other similar meetings, groups, circles and departments, or organise excursions and children's playgrounds, or open libraries and reading rooms, or orga- nise sanatoria and medical help'. 'The organisation and systematic conduct of religious instruction to minors' is an offence punishable under Article 142 of the Russian Criminal Code by one year or, for a second violation, three years in detention. Article 52 of the Russian Code on Marriage and Family states that 'Parents must rear their children in the spirit of the Moral Code of the Builder of Communism... Parental rights cannot be implemented where they conflict with the interests of the children'. The very first point of this Moral Code of the Builder of Communism is 'devotion to the cause of communism' — which, as we noted at the beginning, includes militant atheism. Here we come full circle — on the one hand, citizens are 'guaranteed freedom of conscience', on the other, they are obliged to submit to communist doctrine. In theory, the Communist Party is the ideological vanguard of society, not the legislative or executive organ of the state. In practice, the Party is supreme in every sphere.

An authoritative commentary on the Soviet legislation on religion was recently published in Moscow (*Religion and Law* by G.R. Holst, 1975). On this point, the author exclaimed:

> The law does not forbid the parents themselves to teach their own children religion. But what sort of education is it when some believing parents tell their children that everything which exists has a divine origin, in contradiction to the genuinely scientific knowledge which the children receive at school? In this way there arises a hypocrisy and an inner spiritual disharmony which can cause serious harm to the formation of the human personality.

Something very similar was written by a lecturer at a teacher training college in Minsk (Belorussia), whose article entitled 'Save the Children!' was published by the main Belorussian newspaper on 31 January 1976:

The things that are taught in a believing family and the things that the children cannot help coming in contact with outside, represent two different worlds. The world outside the home is immeasurably wider, more interesting and more attractive. If the parents were the only authority for the child before it started school, in school the child places implicit trust in the teacher. And suddenly she declares that there is no God. It is only a brief sentence, but what confusion it introduces into the child's soul! An impossible burden is laid upon the child's mind: it must choose whom it will believe, mummy or the teacher. A split consciousness is a terrible thing. If the religious feelings which have sunk into a child's soul are not shaken at school, they will become his convictions as he grows up.

In these two quotations we can see the seeds of every trauma affecting the Christian schoolchild in the USSR.

On 6 March 1976 Fr. Gleb Yakunin and Lev Regelson, a priest and a layman in the Russian Orthodox Church, addressed a detailed letter to the secretary-general of the World Council of Churches, in which they laid out some fundamental facts of the Soviet religious situation. In a section dealing with discrimination in education, the writers ask:

What can a Christian in the fifth form answer in a lesson or in an exam, when he reads in a history textbook: 'About two thousand years ago, legends appeared saying that god had come down from heaven to earth and lived here in the form of a man by the name of Jesus Christ. Although these legends were false, people believed them'? (*History of the Ancient World*, Moscow, 1972).

...What sort of position is the Christian pupil in when he reads — and the atheist teacher makes him study — a textbook section under the title: 'The Decisive Struggle Against Religious Survivals'?

Filling the school curricula with atheist content condemns the Christian schoolchild to failure, since it is morally impossible for him to learn and expound the anti-religious principles of a compulsory course. In practice, the problem is usually solved by mutual insincerity on the part of the teacher and the child, but on frequent occasions there arise sharp conflicts which cause severe trauma to the children and lead to lowered marks or failure.

The conflict experienced by a Christian child at school can sometimes be even more direct. Many cases have been documented of children from believing families, particularly evangelical families, being beaten up and victimised in various ways at school.

Higher Education

It is clear that similar problems must affect believers in higher education, too. In this case, the mental anguish may be greater, since the teenager or young adult is more aware of the significance of the conflict around him. At higher levels of education, too, the possibility of expulsion becomes a weapon in the hands of the authorities. The Yakunin-Regelson letter quoted above goes on to say:

> Even more serious trials await the believer at college, where he is compelled to learn the basics of a compulsory course in 'Scientific atheism' ... The inclusion of atheism and atheist principles in compulsory courses at college obviously closes the door to higher education for believers. More than this, the door to a further scientific career, the defending of a doctoral dissertation, is also closed to believing citizens, since an obligatory condition of admission to defend a thesis is an exam in atheist philosophy, 'dialectical materialism', which according to the All-Union Examinations Commission is fundamental to any scientific outlook.

A Christian who wishes to go on to higher education is faced with the choice: either he is willing to keep his faith private, or else he must be prepared to meet the possible consequences of an open confession. Here the different characteristics of the various denominations to be found in the Soviet Union obviously play a role — as indeed they do in most of the situations we shall describe in this chapter. The Russian Orthodox Church, the oldest denomination in the USSR, is a sacramental Church, oriented towards the liturgy, the sacred building, the importance of the ordained clergy, and so on. Adherence to the Orthodox faith can, even in Soviet conditions, be a passive rather than an active affair. For an Orthodox believer to regard his faith therefore as an inward reality, and to remain silent on religious topics unless directly challenged, does not necessarily imply conscious compromise on his part.

The Roman Catholic Church is most heavily represented in the Lithuanian Soviet Republic, where it enjoys a special position as a strong national Church, regarded by many Lithuanians as their bulwark against the Russian invaders. Rank and file Lithuanian Catholics have been extremely outspoken in recent years, and are not shy about religious topics in everyday life. But the Lithuanian situation is not typical of the USSR as a whole. The Lutheran Church, too, tends to be most heavily represented in certain areas, notably the Baltic states, and is thus affected by specific local and national factors.

Much more widespread are the evangelical denominations — lumped together in the Soviet media as 'sects' — such as Baptists (this term refers to the joint denomination of Evangelical Christians and Baptists), Pentecostals, Mennonites and Adventists. These groups lay much greater stress on personal faith and the importance of spoken testimony. Even the Soviet atheist press testifies to the higher level of commitment in the evangelical congregations in terms of understanding and accepting the faith, attending meetings and conducting 'religious propaganda'. Thus the conflict in education, as well as other areas, tends to hit the evangelical Christians hardest.

Here is an excerpt from a letter written by Mikhail Strakhursky, a young Baptist from Kiev region in the Ukraine:

In the summer of 1974 I applied for entry to Lvov Polytechnical Institute. A request immediately arrived at the *sovkhoz* (Soviet farm) where my father works, for a testimonial on my parents, in which it was stated that they are believers.

In the beginning I was not asked any questions at the institute, but then I was summoned to the *komsomol* office. The office secretary, comrade Makar, told me to join the *komsomol*. I refused. Then I was summoned to a conversation with the dean, L.A. Lukoshuk. He told me that I must join the *komsomol* by the New Year or else leave the institute. At the same time he suggested that I give up my faith in God. The deputy dean, I.V. Gaivas, suggested that I come back when I had thought everything over fully. When he found that nothing had changed in my convictions about God, he said that he could not help me and that I was discharged from the institute. When I asked for a memorandum of dismissal, he refused.

Many believers have been dismissed in this way. For example, during an atheist lecture the teacher said that there had been a Baptist girl in the institute, and that 'she got as far as the third year'.

At the beginning of 1976, some leading members of the reform Baptists in the USSR (unregistered Baptists who give allegiance to the 'Council of Churches') composed a long letter, setting out the current situation of their congregations. Under the heading 'Discrimination against young Christians' they noted that:

> Members of ECB Christian families which belong to the Council of Churches are completely deprived of the right to receive higher and specialised secondary education. At first this meant that they were excluded from educational establishments during their final years, under various pretexts. Now believers are simply not accepted for higher and intermediate educational establishments, because they are not members of the *komsomol*. They are not even accepted for training courses.

If this observation reflects a general trend, it means that the Soviet authorities have significantly hardened their attitude to Christians in the field of education.

The trauma of being denied higher education is perhaps even sharper for the new convert. Those who have grown up in believing families have become used to discrimination through years of stern experience. In 1975, a letter written by Pentecostal believers in Vinnitsa (Ukraine) was received in the west. It dealt chiefly with the case of one Eduard Darmoros, who was being attacked in the local media in a particularly vicious way, without any redress. The writers give the following details of Eduard's background:

> Eduard Darmoros was born in 1935. He studied at a special school of music, the Kiev Conservatoire — his whole life was

dedicated to music. Darmoros was an able student and always got good marks. During his time at the Conservatoire, Darmoros came to believe in the Lord. When this became known to the teachers and the authorities, they began to 're-educate' him. This finished by his being expelled from the Conservatoire in his final year for 'poor progress' and in May 1963 being sentenced to five years' imprisonment and five years' exile.

The 10-year sentence was a harsh one. This is possible in the Ukraine, while in other republics imprisonment and exile are alternative punishments. The fact that Darmoros was sentenced to labour camp, as well as being expelled from the music school, was probably due to the fact that Khrushchev's anti-religious campaign was then in full swing. But his expulsion, and its perverse timing, are still typical of the Soviet Christian experience in higher education.

In The Army

The question of military service has sometimes been a controversial one in Christian circles. Obviously the problem takes on a sharper edge where military service is compulsory, as it is in the USSR. There has been a strong pacifist strand in the development of the Russian Protestant movement, and it is still in evidence today, although not on a large scale. Daniil Vashchenko, son of presbyter Grigori Vashohenko, one of the leading figures in the current Pentecostal drive for emigration from the Soviet Union, was recently sentenced to three years as a conscientious objector. His father Grigori acted as his defence lawyer in court.

As in a number of other areas, it is the Baptists who have furnished the most specific and detailed information concerning the persecution of young Christians in the army. In a recent letter, they wrote that:

> Over the last few years, young believers have been subjected to a new form of persecution while serving in the Army. This has to do with refusal to take the oath on religious grounds. Although they do not refuse military service as such, this is what they are charged with. They are then tried and imprisoned for long periods (up to 4 years and more) in corrective labour colonies.

Alternatively they are punished with severe conditions of service in the army which sometimes cause loss of health and even life. At the same time it is demanded that they give up their faith in God. We have endured this silently for a number of years, but now that this type of persecution against our Christian young people in the army has taken on a systematic character, we can no longer look on quietly while our children are being destroyed.

The writers go on to list a number of cases, including that of young Viktor Montik from Belorussia. Here are some excerpts from this story:

Viktor Nikolayevich Montik, born 1952, refused to take the oath on religious grounds. He was sentenced under article 249 'a' of the Russian Criminal Code, on the pretext of refusing to carry out service duties, to 5 years detention. While in camp at Kokhma, he was sentenced again by Ivanov regional court to 3 years' detention, for alleged religious agitation. He is serving his sentence at Kineshma. The administration, first of the camp in Ivanov, then of the camp in Kokhma, tried every possible means to knock faith in God out of Viktor. For the first year and a half, the camp administration tried to re-educate him by flattery, but this had no effect. Then they began to deprive him of correspondence, and the right to use the camp shop for several months at a time. They deprived him of general and personal visits, and frequently put him in solitary for 15 days. The prisoners loved Viktor. But when two criminal prisoners also decided to become Christians, the KGB went into action. They began to fabricate a new criminal case against Viktor. The investigator said to Viktor's father: 'Our country is overwhelmingly atheist, and it is following a logical path towards communism. People like your son Viktor and others are pebbles on that path. But our state is a machine that grinds down those pebbles.'

Out of a number of cases of violence against Christian young men in the army, the most shocking so far is that of Vanya Moiseyev. Vanya was a Baptist from Moldavia, who was called up in 1970. In the summer of 1972, after a campaign of increasing pressure and persecution by his superiors, Vanya was first tortured and then drowned in the shallows of the Black Sea. The story was told, in sober and unsensational detail, in a bulletin issued by the 'Council of Prisoners' Relatives', a group composed mainly of wives of Baptist prisoners. It has become widely known in the west. Although Vanya's murder may be attributed to the sadism of a vicious and possibly unbalanced senior officer, it illustrates starkly the dangers to which young believers are exposed, totally cut off from home background and immediate support. Conscripts are normally sent to areas far away from their home region (this applies particularly to young soldiers from the non-Russian republics).

At Work

The whole communist ideology is built upon the concept of work. Labour is the dignity of man, not his bondage. Honest toil makes a man stand tall, and gives him fulfilment. The right to work is basic to every human destiny. The Soviet labour camps are officially described as 'corrective labour colonies'. The idea behind this phrase is that by being forced to work, rather than pursuing those anti-social activities for which they have been punished, individuals will be 'corrected' in their thinking and return to society as useful persons. In practice, men and women in the camps are subjected to an intense degradation.

It is against the background of this official attitude to work that we must place the discrimination against Christians in this realm. Documents from the Soviet Union abound with testimonies of believers who have managed to obtain a higher education, or other special qualifications, but have then been unable to acquire or to keep a job suited to those qualifications. Discrimination in work is specifically forbidden in Soviet law. Nevertheless it takes place on a wide scale. In many spheres it is an unwritten but clearly understood rule that believers will not be employed. If a person is hired, and later discovered to be a believer, he is liable to various forms of pressure, and even dismissal. This applies obviously to all areas of government or teaching — any position in which the believer would exercise a direct authority or ideological influence over other people, especially young people and children.

At the same time, because of the educational discrimination already described, it is obvious that Christians are being edged out of the more highly qualified jobs simply because they have been denied the necessary education. This process produces a host of 'second-class citizens'. Sociologists are then able to study work patterns among believers and to conclude that the majority of Christians in employment are to be found in the less skilled jobs. The obvious implication of this statement is that religious believers are, on the whole, less-than-average in intelligence. But the argument is clearly full of holes. In the first place, there would be many more Christians in professional and academic jobs were it not for discrimination throughout the system. And in the second place, it hardly befits communist writers to imply that there is something second-class about unskilled labour.

Even believers who are employed in menial work, including those who are capable of more highly qualified jobs, are not exempt from discrimination. Here is an excerpt from a letter written by Mrs. Ulyana Germanyuk, the wife of a Baptist prisoner, in September 1974:

> From my very youth I have been subject to persecutions because I wanted to serve the Lord. When I was studying at medical college, they threatened to expel me if I did not recant. Then I went to an institute; when I finished my course the same words were repeated — and I did not receive my diploma. But still despite all difficulties, a year later I got the documents stating that I had completed the institute. Then a new phase of persecution began at work, where I worked as a vet. During this time I was twice dismissed from work, even despite the fact that I have a large family.
>
> Then I changed my place of residence, but here too 'busy hands' found me again. I was only able to work for a year at the new place. After all that I have described, I decided to forget my education and went to work washing doorsteps. Then I worked as a stoker. Recently I worked as a watchman, hoping that I would not be dismissed, but after some time there was no longer any room for me there either.

It is normal for Soviet women to work — because of the relatively low wage scales, and the high cost of food, it is virtually a necessity for most families.

An important aspect of Christian spirituality is contentment (Philippians 4:11). But even contentment can afford a pretext for discrimination. In 1974, in the town of Dokuchaevsk (Ukraine), a young man by the name of Valeri Andreyev, a drug addict, hooligan and parasite (this is how he himself described his former life) became a Christian. Up to that point, no-one had wanted anything to do with him, not even his mother. After his conversion, Valeri's life changed completely. He found himself a job, and began to support his mother. What happened then is described as follows by fellow Pentecostal believers:

> Valeri got a job as an unskilled labourer. But as soon as the head of the enterprise discovered that he had become a believer, he dismissed him from work. Valeri found another job and began to make application for it. During the medical examination, neuropathologist Anna Khailo began to talk with him. She asked whether he wasn't upset that he had been dismissed from work. He answered: No! She replied that in that case he must be ill. Valeri began to witness to her about the Lord, telling her how the Lord had healed him from a disease that 80% of all people suffer from: the disease of resentment. After this conversation she opened a case on Valeri, diagnosing that he should be placed in a psychiatric hospital.

Valeri was hospitalised from 16 December 1974 until 14 February 1975, and given injections. He was then released home again. Valeri's experience, although serious, was not as lasting as that of some Soviet believers. But it demonstrates the total incomprehension of a Soviet doctor in the face of a simple Christian testimony relating to job situation.

Some Soviet Christians follow literally the admonition of Jesus: 'When they persecute you in one town, flee to the next' (Matt.10:23), although as we have seen in the letter of Mrs. Germanyuk, this does not guarantee escape from persecution. At the same time, the Bible teaches obedience and submission to civil authorities, and the vast majority of Soviet Christians take these commands with full seriousness, despite their recurring bad experiences from those same authorities.

Women

It is one of the boasts of the Soviet Union that it has abolished all discrimination between men and women. Because of the proclaimed equality in job opportunities, it is not at all uncommon to see Soviet women doing jobs that would normally be taken by men in other countries, even manual jobs. This has partly to do with the massive loss of men in the last war, although this is clearly a receding factor. It is also quite normal to see women in the professions, as doctors, judges, and so on. Primary school teachers are almost always women. Women occupy a place of honour in the Soviet media. The Soviet calendar abounds in special days — 8th March is the day given to honouring women.

One might, then, query the repeated statement in Soviet atheist writing that church-going is above all the affair of old women. In the first place, this charge is not appropriate to all congregations in all areas, although it is true that many Russian Orthodox congregations have a high proportion of elderly women ('babushki'). But in the second place, if the Soviet Union knows no discrimination on the grounds of sex or age, then the slur implied in this statement becomes meaningless. It is merely one more instance of the contradictions in official Soviet ideology.

Christian women suffer no less than men in general areas of discrimination, for example at work, as we have already seen. But women are subject to a particular form of discrimination — as mothers. Here is an extract from a recent Baptist document:

> Over the last few years there has been systematic discrimination against Christian mothers with large families. Many of them have been deprived of their awards and they do not receive the highest award: 'Heroine-Mother' [given to women who bear 10 children — *tr*]. Mothers with large families are also deprived of their allowances, which affects them materially. For example, Serafima Anatolievna Yudintseva, a Christian mother who lived in Gorky, has 10 children. In May 1973 she asked the social security department: 'Why have I been deprived of my award?' The inspector replied: 'Your husband is a believer, he was sentenced in 1966 to 3 years imprisonment for religious activity.

The executive committee has deprived you of the award.'
Against Yudintseva's name in the record book for awards to
mothers of large families are written the words: 'Not eligible for
the award'. After moving to the town of Khartsysk, Yudintseva
appealed to the local social security office on 20 January 1976
about the allowance for her 10th child, and the award. The
inspector asked her: 'Are you a believer? A Baptist?' She
answered: 'Yes.' 'You don't get any award.'

The document goes on to mention five other women in
similar circumstances. Discrimination particularly affects
those mothers whose husbands have been imprisoned. It is
especially difficult for them to hold a job, and it is against the
law for friends to help them materially. In fact the Baptist
Council of Prisoners' Relatives does organise large-scale aid
to such families.

Here is another excerpt from a Baptist appeal, this time
written by Mrs. Anna Lubyanaya (Volgograd, Ukraine) in
October 1975:

> Christian women throughout our country, who truly confess the
> Gospel and Christ, are cruelly mocked. Have you really failed to
> hear the groans from the breasts of Christian mothers? How
> many letters have cried out about violence and the brutal
> treatment of believers, and still you are silent? I too, as a woman,
> want to tell you about my life which has been tormented by
> violent men... How many deprivations my family has suffered,
> and I have never complained to anyone — but today, when so
> much is being said in the papers and magazines, on the radio and
> in the cinema, before the whole world, about the Soviet woman,
> my grief, accumulated over all these years, rises in my breast,
> bursts out and cries: What about me? I am a woman too! I have a
> right to that freedom which you have signed, just as much as all
> the women in our country. It should apply to me and my
> fellow-believers. But somehow this is not the case.

In Society

It is a frequent reproach in Soviet atheist writing that
believers are socially passive. Inasmuch as newspapers,
journals, television, cinema, theatre, club programmes, adult
lectures and so on all include atheist propaganda, it is hardly

surprising that many Soviet believers avoid these things to a greater or lesser extent. But it is not true that they are passive with regard to society as a whole. No less common in atheist writing is the reproach that when a citizen falls into misfortune, it is often not the communist collective which hastens to his assistance, but representatives of religion. As one recent book says:

> The story of Yuri S. is a typical one. Yuri was a student at an institute of higher education, who was drawn into the *initsiativniki* sect [reform Baptists — *tr*]. He explained this by saying that at the institute he felt completely superfluous. 'No-one was interested in me, no-one understood me. And life wasn't easy for me. I was often ill and sometimes I couldn't prepare properly for seminars and tests. I was hauled over the coals and threatened with expulsion. In my group I was considered a hopeless dimwit. No-one knew that I had been having terrible pains the day before and simply couldn't work. But every time I went to the prayer meeting, the "brothers" and "sisters" always asked after my health.' (*In Search of Spiritual Successors*, Moscow, 1975).

This type of story is so common that it must point to a widespread phenomenon, causing the authorities much embarrassment. Statistics have been produced to show that many of those who turned to religion at a later age did so under the influence of misfortune and the timely intervention of believers with material help and spiritual comfort. This is a remarkable testimony to the 'social involvement' of Christians in the Soviet Union, despite all obvious hindrances to such involvement.

A book entitled *State and Religion*, published in 1974, proudly declared that:

> Socialist society thus creates all the necessary conditions so that Soviet people should have no need to lower their human dignity in turning to religious charity.

In other words, the Soviet welfare system leaves no gaps which need to be filled by the Church. This proud assertion is clearly far from the truth. We may go further than this, and say that not merely is the Christian Church filling a necessary gap in Soviet social welfare, it is in general acting as a civilising and moral leaven in society. Eloquent testimony to the importance of that leaven has been recorded in the *Chronicle of the Lithuanian Catholic Church*, an uncensored publication that has been operating now for several years, to the chagrin of the Soviet authorities. Lithuania did not come under Soviet rule until much later than the Russian lands. The process of enforced secularisation has had less time to take effect. Nevertheless, since the Soviet takeover, there has been a marked change in Lithuanian society, especially among the young. In August 1973, a group of 540 Lithuanian Catholics addressed an appeal to the Lithuanian Supreme Soviet, which was published in *Chronicle* No. 7. They said, among other things:

> Lenin taught that only practice confirms the correctness of ideas, theories and science. For almost 30 years now the young generation and the whole of society have been educated and conditioned in the spirit of atheism...
>
> What has this lengthy practice of atheist education demonstrated? While before the introduction of atheist education in Lithuania juvenile thieving, robbery, homicide attempts, sexual profligacy were very rare, now they are constant phenomena. Special children's rooms have been set up in police stations to combat juvenile delinquency. Alcoholism, crimes against property, murders, lies, dishonesty and the absence of a sense of duty were never before so widespread in Lithuania as in recent years. We meet with callous consciences wherever we meet workers and officials: in shops, factories, offices, clinics, everywhere. Practice has demonstrated that atheist education is incapable of fostering strong moral principles among the young and that atheist propaganda is unable to alter the society's moral level.
>
> Christian morality, that has passed the test of the ages, that sensitises the conscience, that urges man to assume self-control, to conquer his negative inclinations, to fulfil his duties conscientiously and to feel an inner responsibility for his own actions — that morality is negated and obstructed.

These are strong words, and they may be applied to the Soviet Union on a much wider scale. The attempt to suppress the Church has resulted in a parallel individual and social degeneration. Nevertheless, in the measure they are able,

Soviet Christians still function as salt in their local society. Where they are rejected and repressed, there is a hardening in society that inevitably bears its own kind of fruit. Where local authorities turn a blind eye to Christian activity, there is a softening influence upon the environment.

Within The Churches

The most superficial acquaintance with Soviet society will make it clear that a believer is bound to experience serious conflicts as a member of that society. Still more painful, however, are the conflicts that thousands of sincere believers experience within their own church communities. It might be supposed that in the face of such a hostile environment, the Christian communities would be united and well-integrated. Sadly, this is often far from the case.

'Divide and rule' is one of the oldest principles in the world for attacking an organisation. Infiltration of agents, corruption of members, especially those in leading positions, the spreading of disinformation and rumour are all obvious means to this end. They have been effectively used in many different contexts through the history of man. They have also been used, with some degree of success, by the Soviet (and other socialist) authorities against the religious communities in their midst. Perhaps the most successful strategy has been the widespread demoralisation of leadership within the Christian denominations. This has been achieved by a blend of persuasion and pressure of various kinds. It means, for example, that when the state wishes to exercise pressure on a local church situation, it can do so via the authority structure of that very denomination, thus masking the direct state interference. This is a very serious situation, and one which Solzhenitsyn, for one, has pilloried in no uncertain terms.

Felix Karelin has expressed this trauma in the context of the Orthodox hierarchy:

Here is the bishop triumphantly celebrating the divine worship. Everything trembles before him! He is surrounded by a gleaming retinue of assistant clergy... But here is the bishop outside the church, in the world, and suddenly everything has changed... I am speaking about an inward degradation — about fear. The bishop, just now commanding the fire and thunder of the divine service, now trembles before a common official. How can the human soul bear such a terrible polarisation and not come to doubt the reality of one pole!

The Baptist Church in the Soviet Union still suffers from a split dating from the early 1960s. At that time the state tried to impose anti-evangelical statutes which polarised the tensions already present within the denomination. The trauma of that split at local level has been described, for example, by Vladimir Khailo, a Baptist believer from Krasny Luch in the Ukraine. He tells how the new statutes arrived for their pastor, and how the latter confided to him:

> 'There will be a terrible struggle, true children of God will go to suffer in prisons and exile, they'll be dismissed from work, because they'll never accept these documents. To accept these documents would be to renounce the Lord.' I didn't hear any more. I was sunk in prayer. I begged the Lord to give me strength to remain faithful to Him to the end.

The words of the pastor proved true. But some time after this, the authorities carried out a provocation against him and intimidated him into accepting the new statutes. When Khailo reminded the pastor of his own words, the latter turned upon him, calling for his excommunication. Soon after that, Khailo and others left the registered church to form an independent group. This may be typical of what happened in hundreds of other places. Those believers who worship in congregations not recognised by the state are obviously not affected by state manipulation of their leadership in the same way as the official groups. Nevertheless, it appears that a certain amount of infiltration and informing does go on even within the unregistered communities.

The unofficial congregations are exposed to conflicts of a different and more direct kind: their meetings may be broken up by the police and participants beaten, fined and even imprisoned. In April 1975, believers in the Mari and Tatar autonomous republics appealed to Mr. Brezhnev about violent persecution of their meetings. They describe, for example, how the police attacked a Sunday meeting on 6 April in Volzhsk:

> They broke into the prayer house and carried out a fierce reprisal against the believers: they used force to drag old men and women out of the prayer house and push them into cars, without any sanction for this from the prosecutor. They made a search. They carried out physical reprisals on the street — see the photos. V.N. Kotomkin himself, the KGB captain, grabbed a 14–year–old boy and threw him violently into a car. The boy hit his forehead against the side of the car. Kotomkin saw that he had committed a crime and he quickly got into the car and escaped. There were already three people sitting in the car, obviously above him in rank, who did not show themselves openly, but observed all this illegality. After this reprisal, the believers were taken to the police station, subjected to interrogation and detained like prisoners — some were held for more than 24 hours. Thus one 18–year–old boy was sentenced to ten days, charged as a minor hooligan. Another boy of 16, who was still at school, was fined 20 roubles. Two girls… were fined 20 roubles each. The father of the family was threatened with being brought to court.

As well as being exposed to police violence, fines and short-term detention, believers can also be arrested and sentenced to labour camp (and sometimes exile) for longer periods — three years is a typical term. This applies particularly to those in positions of leadership, or involved in special activities such as children's and youth work, gathering and disseminating information about persecution, secret literature printing. This can affect believers of all ages, men and women, and has done so. The conditions in Soviet labour camps are extremely harsh. They are becoming more and more familiar in the west through books such as Solzhenitsyn's *One Day in the Life of Ivan Denisovich* (also in an outstanding film version) and *Gulag Archipelago*, so that we will not spend more time on them at this point. They have been the subject of a special 156–page study by Amnesty International, entitled *Prisoners of Conscience in the USSR: Their Treatment and Conditions* (London, 1975). This excellent book includes a section on the abuse of psychiatric hospitals. Christians are among those who have been incarcerated in psychiatric hospitals on arbitrary grounds. (At the present time, only two or three Russian Orthodox Christians are known to be detained in this way.)

The attitude of the unregistered Christian groups towards the state and vice versa is often more clear-cut than that of the registered groups. But in both cases, rank-and-file believers are subject to tremendous pressures. In the one case, they know that they are liable to be persecuted in a very direct and physical way. In the other, they are aware that many of their leaders — either their immediate pastors, or their denominational leaders in Moscow, or both — are compromised men, who are extremely unlikely to defend them if they should fall foul of the authorities in any way. Indeed, in some notorious cases church leaders have actively collaborated in the persecution of their own denomination. The agony of these situations can scarcely be imagined by a Christian who has never lived under a totalitarian system.

In Old Age

In some ways, Soviet society is more adjusted to the elderly than that of the west. There is a strong 'veteran' tradition and attempts are made to integrate the elderly into society as a whole. Because young parents are usually both at work, grandparents are often called upon to look after children, and it is quite common for grandparents to live with the second generation. In the Orthodox Church, a considerable role is played by pious grandmothers ('babushki') who, with or without encouragement from their children, exercise a religious influence upon the grandchildren left in their care while the mothers are at work. This influence has been attacked many times in Soviet atheist writing.

Because of the widespread discrimination against believers in the Soviet Union, it sometimes happens that citizens who have reached retirement age show themselves to be believers. Once their working life has been completed, they reckon that there is little left to lose. However, when persecution takes on very direct forms, even old age is no security. Some of those who have been sentenced on religious grounds have been well advanced in years, and it is likely that the conditions of imprisonment will hasten their death.

Nor are the aged exempt from actual physical violence. Here is part of a letter from a Baptist congregation in Slavgorod (Siberia):

On the night of 31 December–1 January (1975) we were gathered for a New Year service. We finished the service peacefully and were beginning to make our way home. On the street stood two people we did not know, who set a light to matchboxes full of matches and threw these burning torches into the air. We discovered the reason for this when we had gone a short way from the house where the service had been held. A group of hooligans, about twelve of them, armed with knuckle-dusters, sticks, military belts and iron chains, using terrible, unprintable language, threw themselves like wild beasts on a group of believers, beating up old people and youngsters and throwing them off their feet.

(After beating up a young boy outside the town…) they started back into the town looking for new victims. But before they got there they found the old man K. Dyck with his wife. This old man of 63 did not realise what was happening before he was knocked to the ground unconscious by a powerful blow to the head. The old woman's heart-rending cry did not stop the hooligans, who had become like wild beasts. They threw themselves on their new victim, the old man lying there helpless, and began to kick him. When the old woman ventured near her husband, she was thrown to the ground with one blow. But again somebody shouted: 'Don't beat the old woman'.

When they had finished on the helpless old man, they moved aside. The old woman rushed up to him and tried to lift him, but without success. She wept and cried out for help, but not one of them moved, although they were all standing nearby. When at last the old woman managed to lift her husband and they somehow managed to stagger along, then the whole gang set off into the town looking for new victims… Meanwhile old Mrs. Dyck dragged her husband to hospital by herself, at dead of night, and only there did he regain consciousness.

The letter goes on to tell how old Mrs. Dyck went with another woman to the police station the next day, only to be mocked and turned away. The boys who attacked these Siberian Christians were not chance hooligans. As the compilers of this appeal show, their behaviour and remarks showed clearly that they had been sent by the police, with clear instructions as to how they should act.

Obviously it requires some courage even on the part of those whose life is nearly over to show themselves openly as believers. Although the greater burden of work and suffering must inevitably fall on those who are younger, old age is still no guarantee of security from persecution. The fines which are regularly imposed upon believers who attend unregistered meetings also affect the older members. In some cases, repeated fines have wiped out an old person's pension for several months at a time. Even in human terms, this is a poor return for those who have given their whole working lives to the Soviet state.

Towards the Future

We have seen how the socialist environment in the Soviet Union affects the Christian believer at every stage of his life. We have also seen that this pressure has not extinguished faith. In fact, it is becoming increasingly difficult for Soviet ideologues to deny that there is a religious revival taking place in their country today. This revival covers a broad spectrum from intellectual curiosity to full and conscious conversions. There is a parallel here with trends in the west: alongside a gradual process of secularisation, there is also an upsurge of spiritual life that cannot be explained in human terms. Because communists *a priori* do not recognise spiritual realities, they are clearly unable to cope with true Christian revival. The only methods they are able to use are those that have been tried up to the present: persuasion, pressure and persecution. None of these has proved signally successful.

A book published in 1970 (*Towards a Society Free of Religion*), despite its title, gave a figure of 26.2% of the Soviet population as firm believers, and a further 21.1% wavering between religion and atheism. These figures are probably no lower than those for any western democracy. Given the particular conditions of Soviet society, they are amazingly high. It has been proven over and over again in church history that persecution has tended rather to strengthen the

Church than to destroy it. It is internal decay and loss of commitment that have decimated congregations, not the inroads of Caesar. A book already quoted, *In Search of Spiritual Successors* (Moscow, 1975) reveals that:

> In recent times, some Christian sects have tried to play on young people, speaking a lot about their 'great historical mission'. This consists, they say, in them carrying out 'Christian feats'. Heroism, say the sectarian preachers, consists in serving Christ and disregarding opposition from those around, from public opinion and so on. Conflict with 'the world' is said to be the real incarnation of 'human courage and heroism' in our day... It must be said that the leaders of the Baptist congregations have succeeded with the help of this kind of demagogy in drawing some young people after them.

It is clear that the future of any cause or nation lies with its youth. That is why the struggle for the minds and hearts of the young is so fierce, as we saw at the beginning of this chapter. But it is equally clear that the battle is not yielding the desired results — many young people in the Soviet Union continue to believe in God, and many others are finding their way to the same faith. Sixty years on, communism has failed to kill the idea of God in the Soviet Union, although it has tried to do so at every stage of life and by every possible means.

In June 1976 a group of 28 Christians addressed a letter to the Supreme Soviet of the USSR, appealing for religious liberty. This letter was unique, not in its content, but in the fact that the 28 signatories represented six different denominations — never before had the movement for religious freedom borne such an ecumenical character. Perhaps no more fitting conclusion might be found for this chapter than the words with which these 28 Soviet Christians closed their appeal:

> We write this Appeal not out of any fear for the future of Christianity. This does not depend on the will of worldly authorities — we have assurances on this count which for us are absolutely certain. The experience of world history shows that all the sufferings which have been inflicted upon Christianity have served in the last analysis to strengthen and purify it. The

experience of our own country in the last half-century also testifies to this.

But it pains us that the present situation of religion in our country is causing serious harm to our nation — and this will become more and more terrible as time goes on. Any sickness is more difficult to cure, the longer it is neglected. The abnormality of the situation of religion is the malady of our society.

The aims on which the present attitude of the state to religion is based were developed more than half a century ago, when the total destruction of faith in God was proclaimed as a realistic goal that could be attained in the near future. But life has demonstrated the illusory nature of these hopes. The influence of religion is spreading, young people are being drawn to it. In these new circumstances we must not cling to points of view which life has totally refuted. The attempt to ignore reality is always dangerous, particularly when it concerns one of the central questions in the life of a nation.

We are not the first to make an appeal of this kind, and we are not so naive as to hope that it will be met with instant understanding. But our feeling of responsibility before our country and before history moves us to express our views in the hope that our word will be heard — if not now, then at least before it is too late.

4

The Spiritual Marxism of Mao Tse-Tung

GEORGE PATERSON

In the present epoch of the development of society, the responsibility of correctly knowing and changing the world has been placed by history on the shoulders of the proletariat and its party. This process, the practice of changing the world, which is determined according to scientific knowledge, has already reached a historic moment in the world and in China, a great moment unprecedented in human history: that is, the moment for completely banishing darkness from the world and for changing the world into a world of light such as never existed before...

-Mao Tse-tung

If he had said nothing else than these words Mao would still have placed himself in a different category from all other world revolutionary figures — excluding Jesus Christ — but including Karl Marx. But the uniqueness of Mao is demonstrated by the many other utterances he made in support of this same vision which not only gives him an unquestioned place in the Communist pantheon with Marx, Engels, Lenin and Stalin, but in his identification with the young visionary Marx of high ideals and spiritual values he might well lay claim to the title, 'Mao the left hand of God', for the 'spiritual transformation' of China which he attempted.

The political symbols of 'right' and 'left' were derived from the positions of the aristocrats and the revolutionaries in relation to the French King, and Mao's place in history will be recorded as a revolutionary Marxist-Leninist with a unique spiritual emphasis. The term 'left hand of God' is a German phrase used when political or economic circumstances have brought about some development that is beneficial, but one which the people themselves would not have arranged. Outside China, Mao Tse-tung is seen as a great man by the normal standards of the West: superiority in the number of battles — ideological, military and political — he won in a long revolutionary career. Mao himself despised these standards. Inside China he is recognised by Maoists as a great man because of the revelation which he brought, more than the revolutions which he accomplished, and it is significant that he wished to be remembered as a 'teacher' rather than a 'commander'.

The world's China experts, Communist as well as non-Communist, have a poor record of understanding what Maoism — Mao's own distinctive principles and policies — really means. Even now, with his death, there is used the designation 'radical' to describe Mao and his followers, but defining 'radical' in political, economic, educational or social terms according to the current situation without any understanding of the unique revolutionary 'spiritual' dimension which motivated them.

Mao was dismissed by the experts as 'only an agrarian reformer' right up to the moment when he took over the government of China. Within two years of his establishing the People's Republic of China the experts said that the new Maoist government would not intervene in Korea, or in Tibet — and were wrong on both counts. In the early 1960s they did not detect his rise to power after a time in political exile. When he attacked Soviet Russia they said the Sino-Soviet dispute was merely a subterfuge to mislead the West. In the mid-1960s they failed to understand the depth of Mao's evangelical bitterness at the expedient Liu Shao-chi's 'capitalist bribery'. And when the Cultural Revolution was launched they never did understand why the 'littlest Red Book' of Mao's 'Three Constantly Read Stories' had the revolutionary impact on both young and old Chinese that it had. In 1975, following the death of Chou En-lai, they were completely bewildered by Mao's peremptory dismissal of Acting Premier Teng Hsiao-ping, despite the latter's well-known cynical expediency and antipathy to the central tenets of Maoism.

'Of all things in the world, people are the most precious,' Mao declared. 'Under the leadership of the Communist Party, so long as there are people, every kind of miracle can be performed... Revolution is a drama of passion; we did not win people over by appealing to reason, but by developing hope, trust and fraternity...'. Mao Tse-tung summed up Marxism by declaring: 'Marxism consists in a thousand truths but they all boil down to one sentence: It is right to rebel.' Not reform, or just tinkering with the system; not revolt, or isolated rebellions against the system; but revolution — 'total change'.

Maoist communist ambitions in China and Asia fall into the most radical category of this interpretation, and any attempt at understanding or confrontation must take this into consideration. The 'total change' envisaged by Maoism is not only of political systems, not only of cultural emphases, not only of social structures, not only of religious traditions — but total change of individual hearts and minds. It is a revolutionary war for the hearts and minds of individual men and women, and the Chinese followers of Mao are wholly confident they can win, for they have already worked out its success in their own third of the human race over the past half-century.

Kierkegaard once said that there are two kinds of revolution: the really passionate revolution, which tears everything down; and the other, bloodless, kind which leaves everything standing but 'cunningly emptied of significance'. Mao chose the former.

Mao was not the only modern Marxist to harness the spiritual dimension to a socialist society. In Italy the Communist leader, Palmiro Togliatti, in a speech in 1954 (1) said:

> ...We have to understand that the aspiration for a socialist society can not only find a place among men who have a religious faith *but that it can also find a stimulus in the religious conscience itself confronted with the dramatic problems of the contemporary world*... (my italics).

But Mao is the only Communist leader to elevate spiritual ideas to a primary place in a Communist Party programme and to make them the core of a challenge to China and the world. It took Mao Tse-tung, as a Marxist, although not in the strictly classical Marxist tradition, to think the unthinkable: that 'the subjective creates the objective'. The idea that mind might act directly upon matter, or that a spiritual (or *non*-physical) reality might break through and change something held fixed for centuries and even millennia instead of being a prisoner of an irrevocable process, to a classical Marxist *was* unthinkable. Unfortunately, the real meaning of the word 'spiritual' — the early Greeks had twelve words where modern English has only one — has been restricted to a rigid, out-dated, other-wordly, effeminate pietism. But it is in the *Concise Oxford Dictionary* sense that I will be using it throughout this essay:

> *Spiritual*: of spirit as opposed to matter; regenerate man (opp. to natural, carnal); concerned with sacred or religious things; having the higher qualities of the mind.

2.

Communism in China in the initial stages did not have much popularity, nor did it move much in percentage terms after being established in power in Peking in 1949. The initial membership of the Chinese Communist Party when it was set up in 1921 was between sixty and seventy. In 1947, just prior to success in the civil war, Party membership was about 2.7 million. In 1950, when it had set up the first Communist Government, it was 5.8 million. That represented slightly over one per cent of the population. Yet, in 1965, speaking to André Malraux, Mao himself quoted *one per cent* as the representative membership of the Party.

When the Chinese Communist Party was inaugurated Mao Tse-tung was a founder-member representing his native province of Hunan, where he had personally established one of the six existing branches of the Party. Yet only four years previously, in 1917, when a group of students met together to discuss ways of saving the country, Mao had given as his reasons for not going into politics, as had been suggested, that 'it needed money and connections'. When pressed for his ideal he declared: 'Imitate the heroes of Liang Shan-P'o'. (Liang Shan-P'o was the name of the mountain fortress on which the bandit heroes of Mao's favourite novel, *Water Margin*, established themselves to fight for justice and order in an unjust and disorderly world.)

But between 1917 and 1921 Mao came under the influence of two people who were to leave a deep impression on him for the rest of his life: Li Ta-chao, his professor at Peking University, and Yang Ch'ang-Chi, his ethics teacher educated in England and Japan, whose daughter he later married. But at this stage, according to his own writings, although he was 'more and more radical' he was also 'confused and looking for a road'. He was twenty-four years of age. He told Edgar Snow:

> At this time my mind was a curious mixture of ideas of liberalism, democratic reformism and Utopian socialism. I had somewhat vague passions about 'nineteenth-century democracy', Utopianism and old-fashioned liberalism and I was definitely anti-militarist and anti-imperialist...[2]

China in 1919 was still in a resentful ferment because of the West's signing over to Japan the German concessions in Shantung. The resentment was partly directed against the West. The 'May Fourth Movement' first broke out in Peking to express this disenchantment and then spread throughout the country. This outburst of nationalism was followed by a nationalistic 'literary renaissance', and it was at this point that international Communism entered China.

The 'May Fourth generation' believed that political revolution had failed in the summer of 1913 because traditional cultural and social patterns had survived the 1911 overthrow of the Manchu dynasty. This analysis was to influence the Chinese intellectuals profoundly, and predispose them towards the Li-Mao concept of *revolution through transforming the thought* of individuals. This was emphasised by Richard H. Solomon[3]:

The strong link between culture and politics in the evolving ideology of the May Fourth generation *produced a unique concept of revolution.* Even as the movement began to interpret politics in the terms of organised popular action based on specific issues as a mechanism for changing society, intellectuals felt that political action would succeed only if carried out in a larger context of cultural change. *From this aspect of ideological development emerged a concept of revolution which, unlike Leninism, interpreted the essence of revolutionary change as a restructuring of thought rathr than just the capturing of state power and subsequent efforts to transform China's largely agricultural economy...* (my italics).

Two of the first Chinese intellectuals to adopt Communism were Li Ta-chao and Ch'en Tu-hsiu. The latter was the real founder of the Chinese Communist Party, though later discredited for 'party deviations'; but it was Li, executed in 1927 as a Communist, who is now regarded as the founder. Together they founded the *New Youth Review*, while Ch'en launched a 'Society for the Study of Marxism' and a 'Socialist Youth Corps'. Out of this group of anarchists, anti-Confucianists and pragmatists was formed the first Communist Party in the summer of 1921. Mao was one of the lesser members, brought in under the patronage of Li Ta-chao.

Writing of the young Mao at this time, Jerome Ch'en, in his study, *Mao*,[4] says:

Mao's understanding of human nature is founded upon Mencius's exposition of the goodness of man, Wang's of man's malleability, the dialectics of Marx, and, above all, his own rich experience in handling men; modern studies of human nature never have formed a part of his scheme. At the time when he became acquainted with Wang Fu-chih's theory, he was also interested in questions of morality (his reading of F. Paulsen), philosophy (his avid reading of newspapers) ... Within this mixture of revolutionary, utilitarian and voluntaristic thoughts germinating in his mind, he found the *New Youth*, the radical journal edited by Ch'en Tu-hsiu, eminently palatable and he read it regularly...

It was the 21-year old visionary Marx — the 'world creator', with his *Weltanschauung der Welteranderung,* 'world outlook for world change' — who so impressed the young Li Ta-chao in China, and, through him, the young Mao Tse-tung, with his declaration:[5]

> He who no longer finds pleasure in building the whole world with his own forces, in being a world-creator instead of revolving forever inside his own skin, on him the Spirit has spoken its anathema... Least of all are we entitled to assume on the strength of authority and good faith that a philosophy is a philosophy: even if the authority is that of a whole nation and the faith is that of centuries...

Mao Tse-tung was born on 26 December, 1893, in the village of Shaoshan, in Hunan Province, the son of a poor peasant who became a rich peasant. He had a strict mildly Buddhist father, a kind mother, two brothers and a sister. Hunan Province had a strong revolutionary tradition and in 1911 the seventeen-year-old Mao went to Changsha, the provincial capital, to further his education. His imagination had been fired by the reports reaching Shaoshan regarding the exploits of one Huang Hsing who had escaped from Changsha after failure of an attempt to assassinate the principal imperial officials gathered there to celebrate the birthday of the Empress Dowager.

In Changsha he was introduced to the writings of the young romantic Hunanese revolutionary of a generation earlier, T'an Ssu-t'ung. T'an had been beheaded by the reactionary Empress Dowager in 1898 at the age of 34 for his reformist ideas. But before that he had been able to produce the first modern newspapers in Changsha, the daily *Hunan Journal* and the *Hunan Students' Journal*. In these and other writings T'an protested against all the obstacles hemming in the old society: the individual selfishness, the hypocrisy of the 'Five Cardinal Relationships', and particularly the formalism connected with the prevailing culture. He attacked the Manchus virulently, while rejecting empty nationalism, and preached universal love and the abolishing of frontiers. One part of his vision is especially important because of the apparent influence it had on the young Mao:

> ...to break out of the entangling net (created by) the pursuit of selfish interests and of official emoluments; to break out of the

net of such vulgar teachings as those of the school of textual criticism and of stylistic formalism; to break out of the net of all (confining) theories and teachings throughout the globe; to break through the trammels imposed by rulers; to break out of the net of the 'basic human relationships'; and to break out of the net of 'heaven'...[6]

Fifteen years later, in his remarkable *Report on an Investigation of the Peasants' Movement in Hunan*, Mao was to outline the goals of his own revolutionary vision in similar terms:

A man in China is usually subjected to the domination of three systems of authority: (i) the state system (political authority), ranging from the national, provincial and county government down to that of the township; (ii) the ancestral temple and its branch temples down to the head of the household; and (iii) the supernatural system (religious authority), ranging from the King of Hell down to the town and village gods belonging to the nether world, and from the Emperor of Heaven down to all the various gods and spirits belonging to the celestial world. As for women, in addition to being dominated by these three systems of authority, they were also dominated by the men (the authority of the husband). These four authorities — political, clan, religious and masculine — are the embodiment of the whole feudal-patriarchal system and ideology, and are the four thick ropes binding the Chinese people, particularly the peasants...

Mao's first article, written in April 1917, a year before he graduated from the fourth normal school in Changsha was entitled 'A Study of Physical Culture', and included the statement: 'The principle aim of physical education is military heroism.' In the article Mao developed what were to become two characteristic emphases: a concern for the destiny of China, and the importance of courage, strength and the military ethos as the instruments of national salvation. 'When we speak of physical education', he stated emphatically, 'we should begin with individual initiative.'

From his youthful, idealistic concerns at this time it is easy to see why Mao responded to the man who is now honoured by the Chinese Communist Party as its first true leader and martyr at 39, Li Ta-chao, who in 1918 was head of the Peking University Library and why Mao who was an assistant librarian there responded to the young Marx. Li was the link between the older generation of democratically-oriented and Western-educated intellectuals of the early phase of China's New Culture Movement (1915-19), from which the first Chinese Marxists emerged. Li was also the first to undertake the task of adapting Marxism to the Chinese environment, combining both into an explosive ideology of militant nationalism and voluntaristic interpretation of Marxism, identifying more with the young strongly idealistic Marx rather than the older pragmatic one.

Li objected to the later Marxist belief in the inexorable workings of the economic laws of history, foreseeing in the East's primitive conditions what Marx could not in the sophisticated West; that China, according to this theory, would be condemned to a long and dreary period of capitalist development. Even before he was won over to the vision of a world-wide revolutionary transformation promised, it seemed, by the bolshevik victory in Russia, Li Ta-chao had come to believe profoundly in the ability of the human spirit and human activity to change the circumstances under which men live.

'When the young have seen the light,' he declared in 1916, 'they should break the meshes of past history, destroy the prison of old ideas, and suffer no corpses to restrict their activity.'

Li Ta-chao, as a historian, had a broader sweep of vision than other Chinese Marxists. He saw in the bolshevik revolution the beginning of the 'mass movement of the twentieth century'.

> The efforts of each individual within this great mass... will be concentrated and become a great irresistible social force... In the course of this world mass movement, all the refuse of history which stands in the path of the new movement — such as emperors, nobles, warlords, bureaucrats, militarism and capitalism — will certainly be destroyed...

But the inevitable conflict between determinism and activism raised by Li in 1919, shortly after Mao's arrival in Peking, had first to be resolved and was to be momentous for the future of China with its profound influence on the young Mao, involving as it did such vital issues as the Marxist view of the role of human consciousness and human activity in history, the nature of the theory of class struggle, and the question of the relationship between political and economic forces. Li rejected the 'social Darwinism' of the sterile determinist, and concluded:

> The roots of all forms of socialism are purely ethical. *Cooperation and friendship are the general principles of the social life of man* ... We ought to recognize that human social life will always be controlled by these general principles, and it can be discovered that they are always hidden in the premises commonly and generally recognized by socialists at any time and in any place. *Not only utopian but also scientific socialism... establish their concepts upon thee premises...* (my italics)

Mao's inherited Marxist vision, therefore, was based upon Li's socialist values of cooperation and friendship, and upon his confidence in the Chinese people and their ability to bring forth the powerful subjective forces of latent 'surplus energy' which, Li argued, had been accumulating in the oppressed, exploited Chinese masses for centuries. The course of Chinese history, for Li and his enthralled student, Mao, would not be based upon confidence in the inexorable and objective laws of social development, but would be determined by the ideas, the will and the 'self-consciousness' of the Chinese people.

The whole super-structure of later 'Mao-thought' is based upon two fundamental ideas developed by Li Ta-chao:

(i)   that the human mind is infinitely malleable, and able to expand spiritually; and,

(ii) that the human will, once rectified, is all-powerful, to the point that 'the subjective creates the objective'.

This is the fundamental difference between Maoism and classical Marxism, a difference so profound that if it is not understood no proper recognition of Chinese Communism is possible. Further, the challenge to religion in general, and institutional Christianity in particular, begins at this point, with the transformation of the individual and society here related to the human will, rooted in love — or, cooperation and friendship — and changing external conditions by means of inward convictions.

Out of his experience of working with the peasants Mao experienced what he described as 'a fundamental change... in the bourgeois and petty-bourgeois feelings implanted in me by the bourgeois schools'; and, he might have added, by traditional Marxism. From the point of view of classical Marxist theory he went to the opposite extreme of not basing revolution on urban workers but on agrarian revolution from the peasantry. In his famous *Report of an Investigation into the Peasant Movement in Hunan* he wrote:

> All kinds of arguments against the peasant movement must be speedily set right... For the rise of the peasant movement is a colossal event. In a very short time, in China's central, southern and northern provinces several hundred million peasants will rise like a tornado, or tempest, a force so extraordinarily swift and violent that no power, however great, will be able to suppress it. They will break all trammels that now bind them and rush forward along the road to liberation... All revolutionary comrades will stand before them to be tested and to be accepted as they decide...

From Li Ta-chao Mao had learned the importance of organising 'the great union of the popular masses' in a revolution, and now he had discovered the key in the peasants' revolts he organised. He wrote in one of his earliest published works, *Analysis of the Classes in Chinese Society*, in 1926:

> Who are our enemies? Who are our friends? This is a question of the first importance for the revolution. The basic reason why all previous revolutionary struggles in China achieved so little was their failure to unite with real friends in order to attack real enemies.

But in order to accomplish his singular vision of a rapidly transformed Chinese society from the grass-roots, Mao had to apply other principles learned from Li Ta-chao and he

evangelically sought to make new converts for his revolution
— from bandits and secret societies, the despised and
rejected of Chinese society. His passionate conviction that
'the subjective creates the objective', that the human mind
was infinitely malleable, able to expand spiritually, and that
the human will, once rectified, was all-powerful — in other
words, that human faith could remove the mountainous
obstructions of centuries of exploitation, tradition, avarice,
and oppression — was demonstrated in intensive campaigns
among all classes conducted in his own Hunan province.

Dr. Stuart Schramm, writing of this remarkable period, has
said:

> The episode of Wang and Yuan has in fact very broad implica-
> tions. *It reflects the accent on the human will, rather than on
> objective factors, which still characterizes Mao's version of Marxism.*
> A little later, commenting on the presence of an extremely high
> percentage of *elements déclassés* in his army, Mao affirmed that
> the only remedy was to intensify political training, *'so as to effect
> a qualitative change in these elements'*. The notion that rural
> vagabonds can be transformed by suitable training into the
> vanguard of the proleteriat is a striking reflection of that extreme
> voluntarism which has culminated in the idea that 'the subjec-
> tive creates the objective'. (my italics)

In that concluding sentence Dr. Schramm himself shows a
misunderstanding of how Mao's mind worked, for it was
primarily because Mao fundamentally believed that 'the
subjective creates the objective' that it culminated in the idea
that he could transform society's rejects into its social
revolutionaries, and *not* the other way round.

With these reformed groups Mao took land from 'the
exploiting landlords, evil gentry and local tyrants' and
distributed it equally among the peasants in proportion to
the number per family. They then lived a communal way of
life. This was immensely popular and Mao was quickly and
widely supported in his small-scale revolutions — whether
his theories on communism were fully understood or not.

It was only a short step from forming these peasant groups
to organising a guerilla force based on recruitment from a
satisfied peasantry prepared to defend their new-found

possessions. From his successful experiences he produced his *Report on an Investigation of the Peasant Movement in Hunan* in 1927. This was not accepted as official Communist policy at the time, but it became Mao's own basic operating principle and later that of the re-established Chinese Communist Party in 1931 when Mao assumed full control.

In the *Report* he described exultantly how his unique theories of revolutionary liberation were being successfully carried out in everyday situations:

> ...The political authority of the landlords is the backbone of all the other systems of authority. With that overturned, the clan authority, the religious authority and the authority of the husband all begin to totter. Where the peasant association is powerful, the clan elders and administrators of temple funds no longer dare oppress those lower in the clan hierarchy or embezzle clan funds. The worst clan elders and administrators, being local tyrants, have been thrown out. No one any longer dares to practise the cruel corporal and capital punishments that used to be inflicted in the ancestral temples, such as flogging, drowning and burying alive... In the places where the power of the peasant is predominant, only the older peasants and the women still believe in the gods, the younger peasant no longer doing so. Since the latter control the associations, the over-throw of religious authority and the eradication of superstition are going on everywhere...

But Mao was still far from being an orthodox Marxist in any sense. If anything he was a nationalist revolutionary, with support even for Chiang Kai-shek's revolutionary aims. What is now often overlooked is that this early Mao was viewed suspiciously by many of his Communist comrades as the most pro-Kuomintang of them all, despite his apparent socialism and coolness to the Russian-approved policy of cooperation.

With the break-up of the pro-Russian CCP group in Shanghai, mainly through the failure of its pro-Kuomintang policies, the leadership of the Party passed to Mao, confirmed at the Tsunyi Conference of 1935. This was not the titular leadership — for example, neither then nor later did Mao hold the post of Secretary-General — but his power derived from his unique and successful ideology, his personal charisma and his popular support.

3.

The Tsunyi Conference was held at a critical time in Mao's and the CCP's affairs. The political commissar of the Chinese 'Red Army', Chou En-lai, had almost been assassinated by Chiang Kai-Shek in Shanghai, and the Commander-in-Chief of the Red Army, Chu Teh, had been defeated by Chiang Kai-Shek in Kiangsi Province. The retreat which was to become the legend of 'the Long March', from Kiangsi to Yenan, began in October 1934 and reached Tsunyi in Kweichow Province at the end of the year. In the first week of January 1935 the Politburo held the celebrated Tsunyi Conference which placed Mao in control of the CCP.

This Yenan period from 1935 to 1940 was Mao's most fruitful period of intellectual growth, culminating in his concept of the 'new democracy' in early 1940. He was confronted with the task of having to start all over again, with the challenge and responsibilities of his new leadership status, and with the Sino-Japanese War of 1935–45; and this combination of circumstances compelled him to analyse the Communist revolution from different and broader perspectives.

The 'Yenan Syndrome', that emerged as a consequence, or the 'Yenan Model' as it is sometimes called, contributed most to what has come to be known as 'the Maoist vision'. This phrase itself is inadequate, in the sense that it can be articulated under the heading of any 'ten headings' or 'twelve principles' of fundamental policy to provide an operational code. Benjamin Schwartz, who has discussed it, has pointed out that the elements of the vision have not always been prominent, or even consistent, and some have even been ambivalent, in a 'dialectic' sense lending themselves to support of quite opposite policies. Yet when viewed in the abstract, there is a characteristic coherence. Schwartz explains:

> Not only has the pursuit of this vision often cut across other goals
> of the leadership but has with varying degrees of intensity

conditioned the manner in which these other goals have been pursued. Some elements of the vision have had an obvious and almost unremitting impact on reality. The enormous energies invested since 1949 *in the effort to achieve the spiritual transformation of the entire Chinese people* whether in the form of 'study', 'thought reform', 'remoulding', 'education through labour', or 'socialist education' is one of the most obvious instances... (my italics).

A brief outline of the chief characteristics of 'the Maoist vision', according to another China scholar, Donald MacInnis[9], would include:

(i)   an overriding commitment to a society united by something approaching a total consensus, and a society marked by a radical collectivism;

(ii)   a unique emphasis on the individual's total self-abnegation and total immersion in the collectivity as ultimate goods;

(iii)   people are more important than weapons, machines or technology;

(iv)   *an enormous emphasis on the power of spiritual transformation* (indoctrination is far too weak a term);

(v)   peasants and workers, once liberated, have infinite capacity for creative thought and action, and could be trusted while intellectuals could not;

(vi)   self-reliance was essential and a moral virtue, whether in individuals, in national or international policies;

(vii)   *struggle, conflict and high tension are positive values and essential elements in the spiritual transformation process.* (my italics).

The Maoist vision was both particular and universal. Particular in that the People's Republic of China was seen as the spiritual centre and source of inspiration and example for people's liberation movements everywhere; and universal in that it postulated a giant moral battle on a global scale between the forces of good and the forces of evil, while that same moral struggle took place in the life of each individual. It was also intensely evangelical, and, as a consequence, became messianic and eschatological, deifying Mao in the present age and envisioning a new utopian age through Maoist principles of world revolution.

Enormous effort on a historically unprecedented scale was harnessed to the first task of converting the then 700 million Chinese people to the realisation of this vision. 'Study', 'thought reform', 'confession' and other techniques were applied on various levels, first to prospective Party members then to the 'people' as a whole.

The transformation of men and women, from being 'self-centred' to being 'others-centred' was fundamental to the success of the whole revolution, and in this conception and campaign Mao not only matched the young idealist Marx but surpassed him and other Marxist leaders.

In his book, *Ideology and Practice; The Evolution of Chinese Communism*,[10] James Chieh Hsiung has described how this was accomplished:

> Tremendous importance, to the point of fanaticism, is attached to ideological work in Communist China today. The Party believes that the key to China's modernization lies in instilling correct-thinking (*szu-hsiang*) in people's minds. *The objective of ideological work is to create uniformity of thought, sentiment, outlook, psychic commitment.* Several patterns for achieving that objective have been developed, including (i) thought reform, primarily administered to cadres and intellectuals; (ii) propaganda (impersonal), indoctrination (personal and face-to-face), and such mass campaigns as the socialist education campaign; and (iii) production-directed mass movements combining psychological appeal ('The Party cares for me'), persuasion ('for the good of the Nation') and rational explanation ('it is good and necessary because...' (my italics).

'Self-interest' is the 'original sin' of Maoist spiritual concepts. It is seen as the centre of the revisionist educational concept from which come such revisionist ideas as seeking scholastic recognition, advancement to schools of higher levels, theoretical knowledge, and specialized training and status. In study sessions throughout the country all students and teachers had to practise 'self-criticism', 'confess self-interest', 'thoroughly destroy self-interest' in order to uphold the concept of 'teaching for revolution and learning for revolution'. Self-interest produced careerism, individualism, professionalism elitism, profiteering, avarice, selfishness, pursuit of fame and privilege. Within a few years the majority of Chinese were convinced that salvation through 'struggle-criticism-transformation' was readily if laboriously achievable *because they had seen the conversion process work.*

Mao's spiritually transformed 'new man' or 'new woman', therefore, was someone devoted to collective life, seeing his or her interest inextricably linked to the progress of all. His or her vocation was to serve the people, to go where needed, sublimating personal desires for the sake of the collective cause even in such matters as sex, marriage and children. One would not maximize personal income, or advance one's own career or remain in the city if needed in the country, or withdraw from family or group conflict situations for selfish personal reasons, or consider oneself as superior, or look down on people from other regions or class background, or accumulate worldly goods, or fail to help others in need. 'Fight self: serve the people' became as fundamental a principle to Maoism as 'Die to self: love others' is to Christianity.

The Maoist vision incorporated the reducing and eventual removal of material incentives for work performed; individual performance and financial reward being offset by the progressive development of non-material and social incentives, when most people would be internally motivated by spiritual values of Maoist Communism.

James Chieh Hsiung in his book emphasises two very important and distinctive principles by which this was to be accomplished. The first that 'Maoism' is not the same as 'Mao-thought' to the Chinese. To Chinese, 'thought' is conceived as the determinant of all action; and 'ism' is associated with the idea of a 'principle' only. The true significance of the 'thought of Mao Tso-tung' is that it is not just the very synthesis of theory and practice (as demonstrated to a degree by Lenin and Trotsky's 'bolshevism') but the ultimate force that welds the two together. The only correct way to understanding the force of Mao's thought is not in the cult of personality, as is so often supposed in the West, but in the true Chinese meaning of thought — the *szu-hsiang* mentioned in the James Chieh Hsiung quote on the previous page. Mao's 'thought' generates 'correct thought' (*szu-hsiang*), and 'breathes relevance into the actual practice of Marxism-Leninism, maintains situational flexibility within rigid operational principles and schemes, translates doctrine into reality, and can sustain people's faith in the darkest hours.'

The second important point made by James Chieh Hsiung is that *szu-hsiang* is something outside the Marxist concept that ideology is only a superstructure of the economic base or sub-culture. *Szu-hsiang* exists independently of the theory-practice framework, and is voluntaristic. For example:

> Many living examples show that there is only *unproductive thought* (*szu-hsiang*), there are no *unproductive regions*. There are only poor methods for cultivating the land, there is no such thing as poor land. Provided only that people manifest in full measure their subjective *capacities* for action, it is possible to modify natural conditions. (p. 138).

It can be seen, therefore, that Mao's *szu-hsiang* bears a startling resemblence to the Judeo-Greek *logos*. To the Jews *logos*, the word, was in itself not merely a sound, but a dynamic thing, the *word of God* by which God created the world, the very idea of the action of God, the creative and illuminating power of God. To the Greeks, *logos* was the *reason* of God, the principle of order under which the universe continued to exist, a purpose, a plan, a design, the mind of God controlling the world and every man in it. The combination of these two streams gave the Apostle John his conception of Jesus Christ as 'the Word of God'. Mao-*thought*, then, is the dynamic spiritual power energising Mao*ism*.

4.

After the heady challenge of such a vision it is necessary to recall at this point Mao's own warning, 'that a revolution is not a dinner party... a revolution is an act of violence by which one class overthrows another... to put it bluntly, it is necessary to create terror in every rural area... proper limits have to be exceeded in order to right a wrong...'.

First, the Sino-Japanese War, and then World War II, had served to blunt the edges of this aspect of Mao's revolution.

But with Japan defeated, Chiang Kai-Shek defeated and the Communist Party installed in Peking, the physical price to be paid for Mao's spiritual transformation became harshly evident. With the Party now in power in Peking Mao called on the peasants everywhere in China to rise up and kill the landlords who had oppressed them, 'not merely one or two, but a goodly number' — although he also warned the supervising cadres against 'indiscriminate killing'. Mao considered this necessary for at least two reasons: one, it brought the peasants into participation with an act of justice against those who had arbitrarily beaten, exploited, raped and killed them in the past; two, it was a climactic act that enabled them to understand that something apparently irrevocable had changed, and that they were now in control of their destinies.

The number of victims in the first revolutionary upheaval against 'the landlord class' was relatively limited, that is, compared with the Russian experience or with what was to come later in China itself. Peter Tang, in his authoritative *Communist China Today*, gives the figures as 'tens of thousands', or about half of one per cent of the total number of landlords.

But one year after establishing the Communist Government in Peking Mao found himself in a war with the United States in Korea, and leading a people who were still, broadly speaking, friendly towards the United States. In launching a 'Resist America and Aid Korea' movement, therefore, he not only had to induce a nationwide 'anti-America' attitude by means of the ideological mechanisms he had created: he also had to deepen and broaden their understanding of the evils of capitalism and the values of communism at a deeper level than had been done until then.

This process was carried out in a series of campaigns over the next few years, under educating titles like 'Three Antis' or 'Five Antis'. The first was launched on the basis of draconian 'Regulations Regarding the Punishment of Counter-Revolutionaries' in February 1951. According to an article of the Ministry of Public Security published at the time, nearly thirty thousand meetings were held in Peking alone within a few months, and attended by a total of more than three million people. This was repeated in every city, town and village throughout the country on a similar scale.

The casualties arising from this period of 'accusation meetings' are still a cause of heated debate. They range from the figure of 800,000 quoted by the respected Peter Tang to the sixty million quoted by the suspect Taiwan sources. Professor Richard Walker in a report to the U.S. Senate Sub-Committee on Internal Security estimated 'that Communism in China, from the time of the first civil war (1927–36) until today (1971) has cost a minimum of 34 million lives and that the total may run as high as 64 million lives'. The same report also gives a quote from Moscow that 'in the course of ten years, more than 25 million people in China were exterminated...' Dr. Stuart Schramm says that a reasonable estimate, in his opinion, would appear to be from one to three million executions all told. He continues:

> If we take the middle figure of two million victims, this amounts to about 0.3 per cent of the total population of China. (It thus corresponds to about 150,000 executions in a country the size of France or Britain, or 600,000 in the United States). This, 'he maintains', is not an enormously large toll for a social revolution of this magnitude, carried out in the wake of a long and cruel civil war which had taken even more victims on both sides...[11]

Whatever the figure, the need for the campaign had passed by the mid-1950s, when Mao considered that the Chinese people had been educated into proper respect for the law under the new regime, that the law was now only 'a terror to the evil-doer', and has never been repeated, even during the chaos of the Cultural Revolution. In 1955 Mao called for a national switch of energies to collectivisation. As a result of this appeal the process of multiplying co-operatives accelerated so rapidly that it exceeded even Mao's optimistic prophecies. Those 'latent surplus energies' of the Chinese people, believed in so ardently by Mao and his teacher, Li Ta-chao, were now harnessed on an awesome scale for the physical transformation of China.

This coincided with the end of the first Five Year Plan and the planning of the Second, the increasing level of industrial development and investment, the deteriorating relationships with Soviet Russia and urgent need for China to acquire its own nuclear capability in the light of this. Ten years later, at the time of the convulsive Cultural Revolution, Mao himself described this period as the critical beginning of dissensions within the Party which precipitated the later Revolution.

Certainly Mao himself designated 1955 in spiritual terminology 'the year of decision in the struggle between socialism and capitalism', in which 'a raging tidal wave has swept away all the demons and ghosts'.[12]

But what has been called Mao's 'revolutionary romanticism' led him precipitately to launch his 'Hundred Flowers' campaign ('Let a hundred flowers bloom, let a hundred schools of thought contend') in his expectation that the spiritual transformation campaigns had converted everybody to enthusiastic communism — including the 'untrustworthy intellectuals', as he had termed them. The criticisms that arose from this freedom, coupled with the economic and other disasters of the 'Great Leap Forward', created such chaos for the Party that Mao, for the first time since his early days, was pushed from the centre-stage of policy-making into respectful but powerless political exile.

That this removal from the centre of Party power was traumatic for Mao we now know from the bitterness of his later attacks on his erstwhile comrades during the restoration period of Maoism in the Cultural Revolution. The standard Party jargon of accusations of 'economism', 'revisionism', and 'capitalist bribery' addressed to Liu Shao-chi for his agricultural and economic policies, and the 'military adventurism' of Lin Piao, were then exceeded by the personal epithets of 'scabs, hobgoblins, demons, bandits', and so on.

The deification of Mao had begun officially at the Seventh Congress in April 1945 when the new Party Constitution contained a preamble in which 'The Thought of Mao Tse-tung' was officially enshrined as necessary to 'guide the entire work of the Party'. At that time Liu Shao-chi, the Party's 'Organisation Man,' praised Mao as 'not only the greatest revolutionary and statesman in Chinese history, but also its greatest theoretician and scientist.' Nor was this all. Liu moved beyond the sphere of pure ideology to assert the claim for Mao's thought, and by association with the Chinese leadership, of a leading place in the world revolutionary movement. 'The thought of Mao Tse-tung', he wrote, '...will make great and useful contributions to the struggle for emancipation of the peoples of all countries in general, and of the peoples of the East in Particular'.[13]

Mao himself, while deprecating excessive adulation, provided the definition of 'the cult of the individual' at the Chengtu Conference in 1958:

> There are two kinds of cult of the individual. One is correct, such as that of Marx, Engels, Lenin and the correct side of Stalin. These we ought to revere and continue to revere for ever. As they held truth in their hands, why should we not revere them? We believe in truth: truth is the reflection of objective existence. A squad should revere its squad leader; it would be quite wrong not to. Then there is the incorrect kind of cult of the individual in which there is no analysis, simply blind obedience. This is not right... The question at issue is not whether or not there should be a cult of the individual, but rather whether or not the individual concerned represents the truth. If he does, then he should be revered...

From 1945 to 1955 Maoism was Party policy, but from 1955 to 1965 his principles were largely ignored in favour of the 'economic pragmatism' which he hated. However, his popular deification was allowed to continue. Edgar Snow, in *The Other Side of the River*, written in 1962, said:

> Today's image of Mao among the masses is hardly that of an executioner. What makes him formidable is that he is not just a Party boss but by many millions of Chinese is quite genuinely regarded as a teacher, statesman, strategist, philosopher, poet-laureate, national hero, head of the family, and greatest liberator in history. He is to them Confucius plus Lao-tzu plus Rousseau plus Marx plus Buddha... Mao has now become an Institution of such prestige and authority that no one in the Party could raze it without sacrificing a collective vested interest of first importance. Probably no one knows that better than Mao himself...

The most popular song in China proclaimed:

The east is red,
The sun rises,

On the horizon of China
Appears the great hero Mao Tse-tung;
He is the great saviour of the people.

Mao's likeness adorned every home, every school, every public office and factory. In many homes his image occupied the central place on the family altar previously held by the ancestral tablets of the family. Mao was compared to the life-giving forces of nature, most especially the sun, and cited as the authority on everything from art to night-soil collecting.

It was inevitable that the 'economic pragmatism' of Liu Shao-chi being practised during the decade 1955–65 would clash with the 'ideological evangelism' of Mao Tse-tung when he tired of his isolation and began his come-back. Liu offered the people a capitalist production incentive of five per cent bonus to workers and peasants. Mao offered them a vision of a New Society, in China and throughout the world. And so began the 'struggle between the two lines': the Liu Shao-chi bureaucracy's 'revisionist line', and the Maoist 'revolutionary line'. The Cultural Revolution which began in 1966 officially ended in 1969, with the defeat of Liu Shao-chi but with the ideological struggle still going on.

From the epic struggle Mao emerged not only as victor, but as Prophet, Priest, King — and Messiah. As prophet, because of his inspired revelation and his charisma; as priest, because he was the interpreter of the doctrine and the representative of the people; as king, because he was the acclaimed and enthroned leader. He now took his place by right in the Communist 'Trinity' of Marx, Lenin and himself — the father of the Marxist revelation; the son who performed the father's will; and Mao who was the people's *parakletos*, advocate, or holy spirit.

Every day throughout China, a great paean of worship and love flowed upwards to Mao — Great Teacher, Great Leader, Great Helmsman, Great Commander — for the revelation which he had brought to the people; not just revolution, but the revelation behind it. And it is significant that it is as 'Teacher' that he expects to be remembered: the Marxist Word made flesh.

The 'Thoughts of Chairman Mao' were not just 'spiritual' but 'pentecostal' and had magical and mythical qualities. James T. Myers, has recorded:[15]

> The Thought of Chairman Mao has been expanded to make room for *fa-pao*, supernatural or magical weapons. Now the enemies of the State and the people are 'devils', 'demons', 'monsters', 'apparitions', 'spectres' and other such supernatural creatures...

The 'Thoughts of Chairman Mao' now effected miracle cures, made youths play games better, people drive cars better, peasants grow crops better, scientists discover secrets better. Women fed lambs at their breasts before their own babies in order to increase production for Chairman Mao. Juvenile delinquent boys given to throwing stones at girls gave up their evil habits on reading the works of Chairman Mao, and wept bitter tears at their belated repentance.

The respected Professor Holmes Welch has described in detail a typical family ritual performed in front of a table, 'on which were placed four volumes of Mao's collected works, and above which hung his portrait,' and went on:

> The first service of the day was called 'asking for instructions in the morning'. The noon service was conducted before lunch, for which it served as a kind of grace since it was called 'thanking Mao for his kindness'. The evening service was called 'reporting back at night'.

During the Cultural Revolution huge rallies resembling Billy Graham crusades were held. Eleven million or so 'revolutionary fighters' from all parts of China 'shed tears of joy' as they participated in rituals of 'mass intoxication and conversion', and were admonished to 'convert the masses' and 'transform society'. These are all literal reports and quotations from the *Peking Review*.[16]

Smaller rallies were held in local areas, very like the usual church services, with a processional, reading of the scripture, sermon, recessional and benediction. One such, held in Heilungkiwng, was broadcast on the local radio:[17]

> After (i) opening ceremonies to the strains of 'The East is Red' and (ii) a recital of quotations from Mao Tse-tung, (iii) a directive

to hold high the great red banner of Mao Tse-tung's Thought, vigorously grasp class struggle, and do a good job on the production of summer-ripening crops... was read... The rally (iv) ended with the song, 'Sailing the Seas Depends on the Helmsman'.

It is common knowledge how important a part the little red book of 'The Thoughts of Chairman Mao' played in the Cultural Revolution; what is not so well known is that the real key to the success of that revolution was a much smaller book, only a small pamphlet actually, called 'the Three Greats' or 'The Three Constantly Read Stories of Chairman Mao'.

The 'Three Constantly Read Stories of Chairman Mao', were not much in themselves, and the foreign correspondents and scholars who read and re-read them in bafflement were no different from the Pharisees and scribes of the first century listening to Jesus and trying to make sense of the parables he was teaching. In fact, the three stories of Mao were strikingly similar to the stories told by Jesus, as were the effects on the lives of those who 'heard and believed'. The three stories illustrated themes of sacrifice, self-abnegation and service to others — or, put another way, faith, hope and love.

5.

In 1927, at the very beginning of his revolutionary career, Mao had said that there were four things keeping the Chinese men and women in bondage and that he and the Communist Party were going to remove those bonds. They were: (i) *the state system* (or political authority), (ii) *the clan system* (or clan authority), (iii) *the supernatural system* (or religious authority), (iv) *the masculine system* (or husband authority).

Probably the most difficult of the four promises to keep was the breaking of the clan system of authority, for this was inextricably bound up with China's immensely strong family traditions. With few exceptions the family was related to the bigger unit of the clan; and through the clan to its ancestral temples, the land and, by extension, to the central authorities in provincial capitals and in Peking. The land, house and tools were regarded as family property, and the deeds of possession were usually in the name of the family, and not of any one individual. Upon the death of the parents the inheritance was divided among all the male heirs, with the eldest son getting a somewhat larger share, for he was the celebrant responsible for the ancestor-worship rites.

The elders of the clan were not elected but were eligible for office on reaching the age of 65, provided they were able to give a celebration feast to the clan. The clan dealt with all matters too large for the family, and thus functioned as a local government. It also owned communal land and with its proceeds maintained the clan school and ancestral hall, the repository of the tutelary family gods of the clan, the scene of the sacrificial ceremonies and the observance of the seasonal rites and festivals. The clan was also the arbitrator, or court, and enforcer of moral and social order. Any individual or family outside of the clan was isolated and unable to make a living.

Under Mao this system has now been eliminated along with all the others, political, social and religious. By smashing all previous state, clan and religious systems Mao threatened the cohesion of the traditional Confucian family unit, but he also delivered it from the evils of that cohesion. To remove the unhealthy emphasis from the Confucian family and make it less authoritative and hierarchical the marriage law of 1950 was introduced, stating that 'marriage shall be based on the complete willingness of both parties'. This freed the women from the domination of the men of the household. (The old Chinese proverb maintained: 'Noodles are not rice and women are not human beings'). Because of the opportunities of working and studying together, it is now claimed that a new companionship has grown up between the members of the family. Edgar Snow has noted the now widespread use of the term *ai-ren* (beloved) between man and wife, and this is certainly indicative of the changed status.

I mention this as an example to help clear up some misunderstanding regarding the break-up of the family system, and the setting-up of the commune, which too often in Western circles have been denigrated for the wrong reasons. The working mother can now leave her children in nursery or kindergarten while she works, watched over by grandparents who still feel wanted and useful. But on the other hand, it should be added that from the amount of correspondence on the subject in newspapers and periodicals, the problems of who does the washing-up and cooking when the working parents return home were no more resolved in Maoist China than they have been in the capitalist West.

But Mao's vision of a 'sociology of the streets', as someone called it, was brought another step closer in 1975. At this time, in Shanghai and Peking, a move to subdivide every residential street into Maoist 'socialist courtyards' was launched. Until then, Neighbourhood Committees had been running street-level political and educational meetings on a voluntary basis. The new 'socialist courtyards' were organised on the basis of a management committee of ten residents, or 'ten-family solidarity cells', to look after the interests — social, cultural and recreational, in addition to the previous political and educational interests of 30 to 40 families in each street.

For example, children committing crimes in China are not held responsible until they are 18, and in one Neighbourhood Council, near Shanghai, three young people were caught stealing. They were reprimanded by showing how they had 'sinned' against society. But after investigation by the neighbourhood committee a woman was found to be responsible for their actions because, it was said, she had invited them to her house and encouraged them to smoke and gamble. The woman, who previously was supported by her husband and son, was deprived of her political rights and forced to do public cleaning work under neighbourhood supervision until she repented, confessed the error of her ways, and demonstrated her spiritual transformation by good works.

The unique Maoist conception of Marxism, therefore, was essentially spiritual in every sense of the word. From the rebirth of the individual to the remaking of society it was fundamentally evangelical ('salvation by faith') and eschatological ('death, judgement, heaven and hell'). In his well-argued *Revolutionary Immortality*[18] Robert J. Lifton, has emphasised this among other factors:

...What all this suggests, then, is that the essence of the 'power struggle' taking place in China, as of all such 'power struggles', is power over death...

A cultural revolution anywhere involves a collective shift in the psychic images around which life is organised. In Maoist China, however, it has meant nothing less than *an all-consuming death-and-rebirth experience, an induced catastrophe together with a prescription for reconstituting the world being destroyed...*

I would suggest that this new community, in a symbolic sense, is a *community of immortals — of men, women and children entering into a new relationship with the eternal revolutionary process.* An event of this kind is meant to convey *a blending of the immortal cultural and racial substance of the Chinese as a people with the equally immortal Communist revolution...*

The Maoist corpus is elevated to an all-consuming prophecy: it nurtures men, predicts their future, and changes the world to accomplish its own prediction; it sets in motion spiritual forces against which nothing can stand. (my italics)

The Thought of Mao Tse-tung is not just the economic doctrine of classical Marxism, nor the political strategies of Leninism or Stalinism, but a spiritual and ethical corpus designed to transform persons and nations and to shape world history.

John Israel's essay in *Ideology and Politics in Contemporary China*[19] maintains that one of the most massive 'discontinuities' between past and present China was the 'ecstatic religious quality of the Cultural Revolution, for whereas the new Chinese intellectuals had been self-consciously secular and iconoclastic the later Cultural Revolutionaries made a '180-degree turn' to the Dionysian cult of Mao.' Israel explains this new 'theocratic absolutism' as the need for 'a symbol at the centre to fill the void left by the Son of Heaven'.

The Maoist vision of Marxism with its primary emphasis on spiritual values fulfilled the function of a religion, and in consequence made Mao 'the left hand of God' in a world which, either by careless neglect or deliberate rejection, has become bereft of high ideals and spiritual values. It thus represents a threat —and challenge— to a secular democracy or an institutionalised Church.

5

Latin America – Where Marxism Challenges Christians To Be Just

CHRIS SUGDEN

While Christians in western Europe pray for Christians behind the Iron Curtain to be freed by their communist captors, Christians in Latin America are seriously discussing, and in some cases espousing, some of the basic tenets of Marxism. Why?

The answer can be short. The western economic block has failed to produce development in any real sense in that part of the third world that has been most exposed to the western economy and to western Christian culture. Christianity in the west has not been effective in challenging the greed and selfishness in the west which has contributed so massively to the poverty of the third world. Marxism is apparently the only going alternative and some theories of Marxism are too close to the poverty around them, and too close to the truth of the Bible for Christians in Latin America to ignore it any longer.

But the answer must be carefully spelt out. Many Christians in Latin America have found themselves working in situations of long-term poverty and almost unalterable injustice. A significant number, called 'Christians for Socialism', have discovered that aid and charity through Oxfam and missionary societies can never solve the underlying problems; charitable aid can only be an ambulance at the bottom of the cliff, picking up the worst victims among those pushed over the poverty line. What is needed is a fence at the top of the cliff. The causes of poverty must be dealt with.

As *Christians for Socialism* in Latin America examine the roots of poverty, they find them not so much in the individual wickedness or backwardness of the individual peasants or shanty-town dwellers, but in the world economic system, by which rich countries get richer and poor countries get poorer. This system favours and is favoured by the ruling minorities in the republics of Latin America. When Christians there ask what justice requires, they can only answer that it demands a change in these structural relationships of trade and power as well as a change in individual hearts.

These Christians are men and women who are convinced the Bible has a unique message to men. But how are they to interpret God's words spoken to nomads and fishermen in an agricultural economy 2000 years ago to dwellers in the favellas of Rio de Janeiro? They live in such appalling poverty because there's no work for them on the farms in the country, no flocks to feed, no work for them in God's map of the world. What has God to say to these people? What does God want his Christians there to do? What does it mean to obey God in an Argentinian shanty-town?

Latin American Christians for Socialism are very suspicious of academic intellectuals who are ready to tell them, 'This is what the Bible means — now go and obey it'. For intellectuals come to the Bible with certain presuppositions. A rich professor who lives in a plush suburban house will tell you that Jesus didn't mean the rich young ruler to sell all he had, but just to be willing to. But someone looking at the story from a different perspective, like Francis of Assisi, may tell you that Jesus did mean the rich young ruler to do just that. Both are coming to the Bible wearing the spectacles of their own culture and society. Everyone has to; there is no getting away from it. We are children of our time. What Christians for Socialism object to is these intellectuals being under the illusion that they are coming to the biblical text with no presuppositions at all. They believe that they have no cultural spectacles and are able to deliver an indisputable verdict on what the Bible means. But that verdict will inevitably be coloured by their social and political background.

A worse stage is reached when those culturally determined verdicts are used to sanction political ideas that have come from their culture and not from the Bible. For example all condemn the use that some South African churches make of their understanding of the Bible to justify apartheid. But the same cultural conditioning has happened in Western Europe. Some theologians declare that you need existentialist philosophy to interpret the Bible's meaning for today because no one can believe in miracles any more. For example the gospel writers tell us that Jesus rose from the dead. But they didn't mean that he rose physically from the dead — instead the disciples thought so much of him that he still lived on in their memories. That may solve an intellectual problem for western theologians. But it creates two more. For the third world Christian it means that God exists only in people's heads and ideas: he cannot interfere in the material world to heal the sick, feed five thousand or raise the dead, especially among your own hungry family. And for western Christians it leaves them in the comfortable complacency that they have enjoyed too long. God does not interfere with their material arrangements.

South Americans feel that they have suffered too long from foreigners who taught them their culture-conditioned way of looking at the Bible. The Spaniards came and taught them about the Kingdom of God. But really to love God the King meant licking the boots of the King of Spain. After they gave up bowing and scraping to the monarchs from Madrid, Protestant Christians came and told them that God would make them free. So they welcomed the entrepreneurs and merchants who taught them to love liberal democracy and free enterprise. They soon found that they were licking the boots of the gnomes of Wall Street and Zurich instead.

The Latin American Christians don't deny that everyone comes to the Bible with presuppositions. People don't stop being Black Americans or Black British, Indian ayahs or Chinese restaurant workers the moment they begin reading the Bible. The biggest mistake is to suppose that we don't read the Bible with presuppositions. What is required is that we read the Bible with the correct presuppositions and ideas about the world and the society we live in.

Why should Christians be concerned with understanding the way society functions? Is it not enough that we should love people and share the good news of Jesus with them? The answer comes in the form of a question — how should we love others? If I see a reckless motorist knock over an old lady on a pedestrian crossing, is it more loving to forgive him and forget the whole incident, or to make sure that he is caught and prosecuted? If a lot of people are out of work, is it more loving to set up a soup kitchen to make sure they are at least fed, or should I also campaign for more jobs to be created? In order to serve someone's best interests I must know how the society he lives in ticks so that I can apply pressure at the correct point to make sure he gets proper help. A meths drinker may ask me for ten pence, but it may be more loving to direct him to the government rehabilitation centre.

Christians for Socialism in Latin America believe that for too long Christians with the best intentions of loving in the world, have failed to analyse the real dynamics of society and assess the real effect of the church upon it. As a result Christian love has been random, haphazard, arbitrary and sentimental. Too often it has been taken for a ride and abused by those in power. They feel that if Christians are going to make a real mark in the world, they must get to know how it ticks. After years of experience they have come to the conclusion that the best explanation and analysis of the situation they find themselves in comes from marxism.

Why Marxism?

At first sight it seems strange that these Christians should choose a marxist analysis. In western minds marxist socio-economic theory is identified with Communist political regimes. And communist governments in Eastern Europe have a reputation for their ill-treatment of Christians. But the socio-economic theory of Marxism is not the same as European communist governments. And it is attractive to these Latin American Christians for the following reasons.

First of all, it is compassionate. It takes seriously the stark economic contrasts and deplorable social conditions in which

some men compel others to live. It doesn't tell the unemployed Brazilian that his poverty doesn't matter and that his
starving children don't matter, that what really matters is his
soul — it doesn't tell him that poverty is just God's will and
there's nothing to be done about it. Marxism tells him why
he's poor, it tells him that he needn't be poor, it tells him how
he can get work and provide for his family, it tells him of a day
when poverty will be gone forever. Someone who tells you
that, loves you and someone who tells you that seems like
Jesus, who told his followers that domination was forbidden,
that none should lord it over or dehumanise others; that he
had come to bring good news to the poor and told the rich that
they'd had their reward.

Secondly, it is relevant. It offers to the unemployed
city-dweller an explanation of why he is poor, and to the
Christian worker a scientific way to put into practice a love
that will be effective in helping the poor city-dweller. Camilo
Torres, a Roman Catholic priest and sociologist in Colombia
wrote: '"He who loves his fellow man has fulfilled the Law"
(Romans 13:8). For this love to be genuine, it must seek to be
effective. If beneficence, alms, the few tuition-free schools,
the few housing projects — in general, what is known as
"charity" — do not succeed in feeding the hungry majority,
clothing the naked, or teaching the unschooled masses, we
must seek effective means to achieve the well-being of these
majorities. These means will not be sought by the privileged
minorities who hold power, because such effective means
generally force the minorities to sacrifice their privileges.
Thus power must be taken from the privileged minorities and
given to the poor majorities.'[1]

Thirdly, it appears to be the only going alternative to a
programme that has failed. That programme was developmentalism. Its basic thesis was that the 'underdeveloped'
countries were in an earlier stage of development which had
already been achieved in the countries of the North Atlantic.
The marks of their 'underdevelopment' were these: less than
the whole population was involved in the chain of producing
goods; they were excessively dependent on producing raw
materials and so were at the mercy of the manufacturing
countries; and most of the population were still tied to small

inefficient holdings of land which meant that agriculture couldn't develop to allow sufficient people to leave the land to work in new manufacturing industries. The 'development' answer was to plan the economies of these countries so that more manufacturing industries sprang up, so that they were less dependent on one or two raw materials for their exports, and so that, with an improved agriculture, more of the population could take part in the producing processes.

The key was to introduce new technology which would require a lot of capital investment. Then more and more manufactured goods would be produced until a 'take-off' point was reached where the economy of the country would turn into a consumer society on the model of North Atlantic countries. New technology and the money to pay for it could only be imported by foreign countries. But investors wanting their money to be safe, required a stable political situation in the countries lest their massive investments be nationalised overnight. The seemingly attractive price of political stability was to be paid for inducing foreign investment.

But the Christians for Socialism claim that this programme was misconceived and has failed. It was misconceived because the Northern countries believed that their development was a moral achievement due to certain conditions of character such as honesty, thrift and hard work, and the free enterprise system. Any country which would adopt these principles and acquire these qualities would naturally develop in the same way. One exponent of developmentalism, Sir Frederick Catherwood, writes 'If the Protestant ethic is taken up in the developing countries which adopt the Christian faith, there is no reason why it should not lead to the same economic take-off as it did in the countries which originally adopted the ethic.'[2] But Jose Miguez Bonino differs.[3] He argues that the rise of the Northern economies took place at a particular moment in history, and was built on cheap resources from dependent countries. One society cannot move through the earlier stages of other more developed societies, because societies develop together. To take but one difference there are now no cheap resources from dependent countries for the underdeveloped nations to draw on.

From a study in Chile, Christian Lalive D'Epinay[4] demonstrated how the adoption of the Protestant ethic does not by itself make any difference to the economic health of a society. The rapid expansion of industry in America and Europe could make use of the spirit of hard work, initiative and thrift encouraged by Protestantism. But in Chile there is no industrial development. Any progress that a converted individual may make through hard work, thrift and honesty will lead him not into the managerial class of industry, but into the middle class of bureaucrats. And in Chile bureaucrats can benefit few people other than their own families. The lack of industry means that individual conversion has no effect on the state of the economy.

What then are the results of capital intensive investment in new manufacturing industries? Brazil has encouraged these for the last twelve years. A forest of skyscrapers in Sao Paulo and super-highways cutting through the Amazonian jungle witness to a spectacular rise in the Gross National Product. But who has benefited and what has been the cost? *Time* magazine[5] reported that in 1974 70 per cent of the population were still outside the money economy in appalling poverty. 41.6 per cent of Brazilian industry is in foreign hands and the purchasing values of salaries has fallen 23.5 per cent.[6]

To secure the political stability for investment, the Brazilian government withdrew political rights in 1964, closed the Congress in 1966, and suspended habeas corpus in 1963. Amnesty International have released figures of 1031 people known to have been tortured and 213 people known to have died in custody under the present regime. Miguez Bonino describes Brazil as a factory of the multinational corporations, with the population a reserve of cheap labour for them, and the government army and police acting as warders.

Those who benefit from industrialisation are the Northern countries and the privileged elites in the Latin American republics. The bald balance sheet of investment in Latin America by the USA between the years 1950 and 1965 reads: money invested 3.8 billion dollars; money returning to the United States 11.3 billion dollars; net return after deducting foreign aid 5 billion dollars.[7] Christians in Latin America can hardly be blamed for thinking that the idea of development is but a cloak for including the third world as the poor suppliers of cheap materials for the rich world and the guaranteed purchasers of technology and manufactured goods from the rich world's factories. Most of the factories and industries are owned and controlled by foreign corporations. The price paid for the use of technology has far outweighed the benefits of its use, and has in fact created more unemployment. For capital intensive technology is designed for societies where labour is expensive. In Latin America labour is plentiful.

The fourth reason why the Latin American Christians opt for a marxist analysis is that capitalism seems to them to be anti-Christian. J. Miguez Bonino writes:[8] 'Quite apart from whatever humane aspects it may have picked up in its later developments, the basic ethos of capitalism is definitely anti-Christian: it is the maximising of economic gain, the raising of man's grasping impulse, the idolising of the strong, the subordination of man to the economic production. Humanisation is for capitalism an unintended by-product.'

It is fundamental to capitalism that firms and consumers should use resources for their own advantage. This is the precise antithesis to the Christian claim that resources are to be put to the service of all mankind. Capitalism institutionalises human selfishness. It cannot be claimed that capitalism is ethically neutral, that it is a servile economic system that depends for its ethics on how it is used. E.F. Schumacher writes: 'No system or machinery or economic doctrine or theory stands on its own feet: it is inevitably built on a metaphysical foundation, that is to say upon man's basic outlook on life, its meaning and purpose.'[9] J.M. Keynes, one of the modern theorists of capitalism recognised this. 'The time is not yet for a return to the most sure and certain principles of religion and traditional human virtue — that avarice is vice and that the exaction of money is a misdemeanour and that the love of money is detestable. For the foreseeable future we must live as if fair is foul and foul is fair.'[10]

While Christians would be the first to recognise that no machinery or system can eradicate man's selfishness, perhaps they ought to examine carefully whether to promote a system that encourages selfishness or discourages it. R.H.

Tawney wrote: 'What it (a change of system) can do is to create an environment in which these (egotism, greed and quarrelsomeness) are not the qualities that are encouraged. It cannot secure that men live up to their principles. What it can do is to establish their social order upon principles to which, if they please, they can live up and not live down.'[11]

It is often argued that there is an internal brake in the capitalist system that protects the population from excesses such as child labour. South Americans would reply that those excesses have now been exported to the third world. No longer do children climb chimneys in Britain, but they still climb coffee trees in Brazil. And in Britain social developments have not been motivated by an internal brake in the capitalist system. They have been motivated by the nonconformist conscience, they have been obtained by sustained social conflict, and they have been paid for by the discovery and exploitation of the resources of the third world.

The capitalist system has deeply affected the internal life of the Latin American republics. Foreign economic interests have recruited powerful elites whose well-being depends on promoting foreign interests. Press and radio transmit the lifestyle and values of a consumer society. So the population as a whole becomes restless for the goods of a consumer society it cannot yet have. The effect of demonstration of a more luxurious life makes those who cannot have it more discontented with their lot. Thus societies which ought to be working together for a fuller life are led to develop the habits and concerns of a leisure and consumption orientated world. The few who can escape the deprivation of the many are not encouraged to love and help their less fortunate neighbours.

Latin American Christians are forced to the conclusion that the misery they see created by western development is almost to be expected given the operation of the capitalist system in promoting that development. They cannot see any change coming from the leaders of their society, who have been caught in the development mesh and would have too much to lose by a change. What can be done to love the dispossessed and deprived in a practical way? Help involves understanding the causes of the poverty that appals them. The causes they find through a marxist analysis of wealth and poverty.

The Marxist Analysis

There are many variations of Marxism in the world, but certain features are constant.[12] Marxism is a social analysis which claims that everything in society is conditioned by the way that society produces and shares out food, goods and wealth. Men become men, they rise above the animals, by the way they subdue nature. And the way they subdue nature in their work determines what they think and believe.

If the way a man works is creative and positive, he will become a true human being at one with himself and other people. If he can enjoy and use what he makes or receive its full worth from those he makes it for, then he will be a happy man and content with his work.

If on the other hand the way he works does not allow him to enjoy and use what·he makes or receive full worth from others, then he will be alienated from his work and from other people. He will not become a fully developed human being.

A capitalist system alienates a man from his work in the following way. Suppose one man has £1000 worth of raw materials. He hires another for £50 to use his skill to turn those raw materials into finished manufactured products. At the end of the job he sells the finished products for £2000. Taking all his costs into account he makes a profit of £250. The worker is paid £50 for work worth £250, and has been robbed of £200 worth of his work.

As a result the worker feels his work is an enemy. For it is the means whereby a more powerful man than he robs him. His hirer is an enemy, though he be a very pleasant and kind man, for he robs him. His next door neighbour, another worker, is an enemy, because he works for a competitive firm, or is competing for the same job. The whole process of work ceases to be something in which a man can work with others to produce something he can enjoy and use or offer in service. Instead it becomes merely a means to fill his belly and the bellies of his family. And life becomes one continual struggle to achieve greater superiority to others in the possession of property.

The solution according to Marxism is to reorganise work so that everybody has a share in the decisions regarding production, a part in the processes of production, and an equal share in the results of production. This is expressed in many ways — redistributing land to very poor people, ensuring that office workers spend some time in manual work each year, and cutting differentials in income by working from the basis of 'from each according to his ability, to each according to his need'. Because the powerful have vested interests in keeping things as they are, such a solution will only come through political power being given to the poorest classes by revolution.

The structure of the means of producing goods and sharing wealth determines all other factors in life. Religion is merely a means whereby men seek to tolerate or escape from their alienation rather than solve it. They project their hopes for a better life to a world beyond the grave. With this opium for their pain, they are prevented from dedicating themselves to taking effective action against their exploitation in the present. People in positions of power support religion because it serves to justify the present order as an order decreed by God. The people in the labour force are kept in check by their own internal consciences out of submission to God's decrees. So there is no need for the holders of power to make showy use of the army. Religion teaches men to love their slavery.

Action

The Latin American Christians for Socialism are more interested in action for the poor than a marxist analysis of the situation for its own sake, for two reasons. First of all, the marxist analysis appeals to them because it offers an explanation to their heads of what burdens and vexes their hearts. The scandal of poverty and exploitation, which others not only tolerate but cause, moves them to seek effective corrective action. This action is commitment to the cause of the poor. The marxist analysis offers them a tool to analyse the situation in order to act.

Secondly, the marxist analysis can be criticized only in action. Since it claims to be scientifically and historically true, it cannot be properly criticized from a theoretical standpoint.

A particular project is open to criticism only as regards putting into practice the conclusions of the analysis. And that is possible only if you accept the analysis and are actually taking part in the process of putting its conclusions into effect.

Some commitment to action comes before theory, discussion, reflection and theology. Therefore when these Christians turn to the Bible for what it has to say, it is not in order to decide whether Marxism is right or wrong, but to apply what the Bible says to the world within the context of a marxist analysis. Action, or 'praxis' — a Greek word for action, taken by the Christians for Socialism — comes before theory. Act before you theorize because there is no alternative to siding with the oppressed in their struggle. Or, in more recognisable terms, don't just sit there talking about it, do something.

Can Christians be marxists?

What shall we make of our Christian friends who see Marxism as an ally? Can Christians be marxists too? Can there be a useful discussion between Christians and marxists or are marxists totally and necessarily anti-Christian in all their views? How much do Christianity and Marxism share and where do they differ?

They share many assumptions about man and his history. Man is a worker. For Marx man is marked out by his work; it is this that differentiates him from matter. Through his work man not only creates other things, he also creates himself. If the way men's work is organised goes wrong, then men suffer in a very deep way. The Bible shows that man was created to work, to subdue the creation. As man masters the world and uses it properly he fulfils his true role, he finds himself. And if the way work is organised goes wrong, men suffer. It was not God's will for the Hebrews to be slaves in Egypt, for wage labour to be bought and sold in Israel.[13] Work is to be a shared enterprise, and a means of serving others, not a method for obtaining power over people.[14] And all work, especially manual work, brings dignity to man. Jesus and Paul were manual workers, and laziness and 'the idle rich' are heavily condemned in Proverbs.[15]

Secondly, men should not be exploited. They have an important value. Marx wrote out of deep concern for what he saw as blatantly immoral and unjust treatment of men by their fellow creatures. Latin American Christians for Socialism are moved by a deep care for the oppressed. And the Bible displays the same care for the oppressed. Jesus identified the poor, naked, hungry, and prisoners of all ages, cultures and times, of all beliefs or none, as his brothers. The Old Testament kings were called especially to weigh in on the side of those who were defenceless and most likely to suffer from the powerful. Justice in the Bible is not indifferent fairness. It is positive help to the disadvantaged.

Thirdly, there is a purpose and goal in man's history. For Marx that goal is that men should be able to live together with injustice and exploitation. That goal is reached as men themselves alter the methods by which they produce and share goods. Man is not a creature of fate, he is not a prisoner of circumstances. He is an agent. In the Bible man is free from powers of fate and can be freed by God from slavery to powers that should have no call on him, the powers that result from his rebellion against God. The goal of history is when these powers are finally defeated, and when all creation serves its King. For the present man finds his true self in obeying God and taking effective action on the world around him. He is accountable for his actions and is a responsible agent.

Man's material life matters. In Marxism man's bodily and material life is not an illusion, it is not a lower form of existence to his 'intellectual' life. And the Bible does not subscribe to the Greek way of thinking that separates man into a higher soul and lower body. Man's bodily and material life in this world is of great importance. For Marx and the Bible man is a being who can effect significant changes on his situation and destiny in this world. Man's actions and history matter.

There are important assumptions about man, his work and his history that Christianity and Marxism share. Marxism also highlights certain facets of man's social life that Christians may have overlooked in the Bible. For Marx learning and knowledge comes through action: 'Philosophers have spent too long in trying to understand the world, the point is to

change it.' Knowledge comes not through intellectual knowledge, but through taking part in the struggle for liberation.
Jesus focused on the need to demonstrate the reality of faith
through works. For him understanding came through obedience. 'If any man chooses to do God's will, he will find out
whether my teaching comes from God or whether I speak on
my own' (John 7:17).[16]

Marxists speak of man's alienation through patterns of
work that oppress him. Christians see this as an expression of
sin, of man's rebellion against God that divides him from
other men and prevents him loving his neighbour. Christians
would argue that alienation through work is not man's
fundamental alienation, but that it is a very important
expression of his fundamental alienation from God.

Marxism draws attention to the need to change some
structures in order to bring people true freedom. In the Bible
we find God delivering the Hebrews from the structure of
slavery in Egypt, ànd we find Paul declaring that the structure
of divisions between Jews and Gentiles has been overcome in
a new structure, the Christian church.[17] Within the church
the new relationship between men is not compatible with the
old relationships of master-slave. 'In Christ is neither male or
female, Jew or Greek, slave or free.'[15]

For Marxism the goal for man is a society where injustice is
at an end, and people rule themselves. The Bible speaks of the
kingdom of God where all suffering will be at an end. Jesus
announced that the invasion of this world by the kingdom
had begun through him, as he had been appointed by God to
preach good news to the poor, to proclaim freedom for the
prisoners and recovery of sight to the blind and to release the
oppressed.[19]

But there are major differences between Christianity and
Marxism. To be a marxist is to be totally committed to an
analysis of history and society and to a programme of change
based on that analysis. It is to believe that a sufficient
explanation of the conflicts between men is the method of
organising production and sharing of goods: and that sufficient cure will emerge when the structure has been changed.
It argues that a complete explanation of evil is the organisation of the structures of labour, that this evil is temporary and

can be removed by man's own efforts. When the structures are changed, all conflict will be at an end, and all religion which has been man's compensation for a rotten life on earth will disappear. By his own efforts man will remove evil and God. Marxism is necessarily atheistic.

Though it shares many assumptions about man and his history with Christianity, it trades on those assumptions rather than justifies them. For example, Marxism argues that the present structures of capitalism are wrong, they should be changed and the conflicts they cause should be ended. The reason is that capitalism is destined by history to disappear. It should go because it will go, not because it is an unjust system and ought to go. To call something unjust involves an objective moral judgement. And on a marxist view, such judgements are impossible; moral judgements merely reflect the subjective views of men who are determined by their position in the economic and class structures of their society.

But history has not moved in the direction that Marx predicted. Capitalism has not disappeared. But will it? (At least not in the way forecast by classical Marxism). So all we have left is a moral argument against the grave injustices of the capitalist system. But within Marxism there are no grounds for making a moral choice. We may fairly ask, 'Why side with the oppressed, why not join with the oppressor? Why remedy the situation at all?' To move from a marxist analysis of the economic facts of life to a programme for change depends on a moral judgement that Marxism is unable to sustain. In terms of television programming, Marxism may be said to offer us an analysis of 'The Financial World Tonight' and follow it with a devotional 'Epilogue'. But it has in fact no moral basis for offering us an epilogue on the need and method for changing the world at all.

In this instance Marxism trades on the validity of making a moral judgement, without being able to sustain it. It also makes a number of particular moral judgements about the importance and value of work, the care of the poor, and the satisfaction for men if they are not alienated from their work. Yet it can offer no basis for them. Marxism argues that there is a purpose and goal in history which will be reached as man is perfected. But what grounds does it give for believing there is a purpose within history? Marxism holds that man's conflicts derive from the capitalist system of labour, where economic self-interest becomes a virtue. But where did men get the idea that they would be happier by being selfish than by being unselfish? Marxism on its own cannot be a total explanation of our human situation.

Marxism doesn't prove enough. But Marxism also proves too much. In holding that all value systems, religion, ideas and political theories are the immediate consequence of man's economic situation, it not only denies itself any basis for moral judgement, but it is in danger of excluding itself. For Marxism is arguably also a theory conditioned by the economic situations of its supporters and so of no final scientifically objective status.

Evaluation

Marxism claims to be a total explanation of human life; and it is a necessarily atheistic explanation. So Christians cannot be Marxists in a full-blooded sense. But the marxist analysis of the workings of capitalism are not dependent on the marxist philosophy of history. The fact that Marx's historical projections that history will inevitably see the end of capitalism have not worked out is no case for ignoring the economic analysis that he offers. The fact that many attempts to follow through the consequences of his analysis have brought efficiency and a measure of economic success to marxist states at the high price of conformism and military discipline should also not blind us to the realities marxist analysis exposes. It is the price that has been paid for change, rather than the need and benefits of change that is most regularly challenged.

So there are no moral or religious reasons why, as an economic analysis of the base and performance of capitalism, the marxist analysis should be rejected by Christians. The Bible does not claim to give an exhaustive account of the workings of human society, and if Marxism highlights the truth in some areas, Christians have no cause to reject it. Christians can learn from the marxist analysis of economics and social history. This analysis may make them ask ques-

tions of scripture which otherwise they would not have
thought of putting. And they can offer the marxist a more
satisfactory account of the origin and solution to evil.
Marxists can help Christians apply Christianity and Christians can help marxists move beyond Marxism.

Understanding the Bible

Christians for Socialism argue that Christians often shield
themselves from what the Bible actually does say because
they are unaware that they are reading it through the
spectacles of their own culture and world picture. So to take a
crude illustration, Christians with excessively individualist
views have failed to understand that Paul's injunctions to
'you' in his epistles are to a group of people and not just to an
individual. The Christians for Socialism argue that we need
the correct understanding of our contemporary world in
which to apply the Bible. Does the Bible help us move beyond
Marxism in gaining a correct understanding of that world? If
we drop the spectacles of our own culture does the Bible itself
provide us with the correct ones?

The Bible's understanding of evil and world history is not
of a process moving inevitably under its own steam to a
utopia, as in Marxism, but of two ages of man. There is the old
age, where all men are locked in rebellion against God and
against God's will. One of man's fundamental commands
from God was to be ruler in God's place of all that was on the
earth, its resources and its creatures. Man was to dominate
everything on earth, except other men. But in the fall man
committed himself to living outside God's presence. One of
the consequences of this was that man began to dominate
man. Other consequences led to the break-up of human
relationships, the spoiling of the physical world through
disease and disaster, and the final consequence was physical
and spiritual death. Man in the old age is locked in a totally
closed system whereby however he might rearrange the
furniture, he can never escape the prison of evil. Man on his
own cannot so reorder his social relationships that all evil is
eradicated and all men have equal freedom. The history of
marxist revolutions has proved this once more.

Into this old age a new age has invaded. Into this kingdom of darkness, the kingdom of light has come. Into the kingdom of Satan has burst the kingdom of God. The kingdom of God is where God rules and is Lord. The kingdom comes to redeem creation, the kingdom expresses the Lordship of God. And this rule is exercised in Christ.

The kingdom has two poles. It has a future pole. The hope of the kingdom began with the Jews. God's purpose for them had been that they should be a light to the nations to show through their life-style what God was like. Their history was to be a film-show through which the nations would understand the character and the opinions of the great unseen director. It became painfully clear that the people of Israel were unable to live up to this calling and responsibility. To clear his own name God judged the social injustice, immorality and oppression that the Israelites had allowed to grow unchecked in their society. But all was not lost. God promised that he would intervene to create a new world where his people would be the proper light they were meant to be, and other nations would be drawn to God through that light. So deep was the disease of man's rebellion and evil that such a project would demand a new spiritual sphere and a new physical sphere. Isaiah saw a renewal of creation, with the blind and the deaf being healed — he saw peace and justice among the nations. Jeremiah saw a new relationship between God and man, a new covenant. Joel saw God pouring his Spirit out on all classes and groups of people. Ezekiel saw the forgiveness of sins and a new, and just, shepherd-king for Israel. For those who had been faithful to God to enjoy this wonderful new world, some foresaw in faith the resurrection of the dead.[20]

Jesus proclaimed that he was God's agent to bring this kingdom into history ahead of schedule. His message was, 'The time is fulfilled, and the kingdom of God is at hand; repent and believe the good news.' To the Pharisees he made clear that his exorcisms meant that the kingdom of God had invaded to defeat the powers of evil.[21] To John the Baptist he made clear that his healings were a demonstration that God was renewing his creation through him.[22] So Jesus gave the kingdom a second pole, a present pole. His good news was that it wasn't necessary to wait to the end of the world to experience God's defeat of evil and his new order. Now that order had invaded human reality and men could enter it now. Of course Jesus also looked forward to a time when the kingdom would come in its fulness. He taught his disciples to pray, 'Thy kingdom come'; he spoke at the end of his ministry of the arrival of the Son of Man in his kingdom to judge the nations of the world; he spoke at the last supper of eating with his disciples in the kingdom of God.

What would the kingdom of God look like? Jesus described it in terms of new relations with God, with fellow men and with the physical world. There would be a new relation with man and God; men could call God 'Abba', Father. Their sins would be forgiven. But if their sins were forgiven they were to forgive their fellow men their sins too. So Jesus brought new relations between man and man, expressed also in his involvement with the hated Samaritans, his care for the traitor tax-collectors, and his compassion for women whom he liberated from being second-class citizens in his company. There would also be new relations with the physical world. His healings demonstrated that God would renew the physical aspect of man's life, and the resurrection showed that this would mean the resurrection of man's bodily existence.

The invasion by God's kingdom means that the power of evil to have the last say over men was broken. Jesus spoke of the strong man being bound and his goods being spoiled. Jesus promised the gift of the Spirit to alter fundamentally the direction of man's will and aspirations. Paul developed Jesus' teaching by speaking of men being new creatures in Christ, risen from the old age to a new level of life in the new age, resurrection life, the life of the kingdom of God.[23]

Moving beyond Marxism

What are the implications of this theological framework of the kingdom for the encounter of Christians with marxists? It gives Christians a vocabulary for understanding the economic order. One reason why Christians have almost totally identified with Marxism is that the Christian Church has failed to provide a vocabulary or a theology for understanding economic order and justice, or has even denied that it was possible. It allows Christians to make positive use of what is true in Marxism. Just as Christians make full use of the analysis of science in everything from motor-car engines to medicine, so they can make full use of the economic analysis of Marxism where this is correct. And it gives Christians principles for moving beyond Marxism in solving the injustices they see; these do not trade off the marxist imagination or framework, they are derived from the most basic theological premise in their scriptures, the rule of God.

The vocabulary and the framework of the kingdom of God enable Christians to make proper use of the marxist analysis to identify and name injustice in society that expresses rebellion against God. While Marxism doesn't give a total analysis of evil, it nevertheless can be used as an acceptable description of the effects of evil in the old age. In biblical times writers identified the way in which rebellion against God showed itself. In the New Testament we see racial separation; idolatrous politics, where the emperor demanded worship; and legalistic religion, roundly condemned as showing rebellion against God. In the exodus story oppressive slavery is shown to be inconsistent with God's will for men; in the prophets excessive luxury is likewise condemned. Jesus himself opposed the domination of man by man, and luxury that was content to live in wilful ignorance of the poor. In our society today rebellion against God appears as greed, a lust for power, the desire to compete against and dominate others (those in favour of competition are always those who win the competitions), which are all expressed in the pursuit of increasing consumption. God's will for his people has always been to live in obedience to him against the prevailing rebellion of the times. Insofar as Marxism correctly reports the facts of our world or coincides with the logical consequences of the biblical message, Christians should listen to it and change their personal and political practice.

For Marxism shows the unjust economic stratification of present society, where the rich get richer and the poor poorer. Even in Britain those with the most satisfying jobs have the highest incomes, the best places to live, and access to alternative forms of education. Both Marx, and the Bible (in the equal society of early Israel) would favour the system of payment: 'from everyone according to their ability, to everyone according to their need'. The Bible shows this matters— for in the society that grew out of Pentecost, the disciples shared their goods that none should go in want. This did not prove a failure — for Paul's collection was to help in a time of *famine*, not because the Christians had run out of capital. And it just is not the case that people work only for high wages. Consider nurses, teachers, cleaners, tea ladies and the night watchman. The executive's plea for a yet higher salary (that if you pay people peanuts you get monkeys) is an insult to most working people who earn less than he does.

Christians have no reason to dispute Marxism's description of the alienating character of work under any kind of capitalist system, or its description of the necessary relationship between the expansion of the capitalist nations and the poverty of the third world. That relationship has been proved time and time again at UNCTAD conferences and by many economic reports.

Christians in the west should listen hard to the condemnation of the blind pursuit of an ever increasing consumption of things as the inevitable fruit of a free enterprise society; to the observation that the vested interests of the dominant classes are a decisive influence on much human culture; to the critique of the notion of private property and freedom in capitalism.

Capitalism is founded on the notion that the fruits of one's investment are entirely at one's own disposal, whereas the Bible urges that all goods are held in stewardship for the service of others. The theory of surplus value correctly describes the way the labour of the worker benefits only the one who can afford to hire him, and of necessity creates conflict between worker and employer. This falls far short of the biblical picture of work as a shared enterprise in which man co-operates with man.[24] The structure that Marxism suggests where the means of production are owned jointly by all concerned does not necessarily mean nationalisation and does not necessarily mean inefficiency E.F. Schumacher correctly points out that free enterprise can be equally inefficient.[25] The crucial point is one of size and responsibility. Medium-scale operations, in which decisions and profits are shared among workers and representatives of local bodies where the firm is situated, would channel the products and profits of industry to the benefit of the workers and residents immediately affected by them, and not merely those who invest their money but not their lives or homes into the business of the company.

If Marxism has exposed the facts which demonstrate that capitalism has not solved the problem of poverty in the industrial countries, but has merely exported it to third world countries, then Christians have no Christian brief to fly in the face of truth.

Before trading relationships were set up at the beginning of the last century between the mercantile nations of the west and their colonies, poverty in the latter countries was infinitely less than it is today. On a global scale industrialization and the accumulation of wealth have paradoxically accumulated poverty — because the wealth has been concentrated unequally.

Least of all have Christians the right to cover up these glaring social sins by saying that they don't really matter; all that matters is that souls are saved for eternity. Time and again in the Old Testament God denounces religion that covers up glaring social injustices. The temple was never better supported than when Isaiah began prophesying. But his word from God was: 'Your new moons and your appointed feasts my soul hates; they have become a burden to me, I am weary of bearing them... seek justice, correct oppression, defend the fatherless, plead for the widow.'[26] When their moral practices showed that their religion was vain and empty, God on two occasions destroyed the very symbols of his presence among the Jews, the temple and the altar of sacrifice. Jesus made very clear that it was impossible to call him 'Lord, Lord' without doing the things he said — which included feeding the hungry, healing the sick, caring for prisoners and clothing the naked. These he described as 'his brethren' — he identified himself with the poor and oppressed throughout his ministry, especially the people of the land, whom the Pharisees, the Sadducees, the Essenes and the Zealots were content to call 'cursed by God'.[27] Jesus was not a Greek who believed the soul was more important than the body — he was a Hebrew whose only hope for a life beyond the grave was for a resurrected body. And Jesus' demonstration of the reality of the invading kingdom was not just shown in forgiving men their sins, but also in feeding their bodies, healing their diseases, and shattering some of the oppressive social conventions such as keeping women and children away from men's presence, separation from Gentiles and law-breakers, and refusing to do good works on the sabbath.

But where does the message of the invading kingdom bite on the problems of evil in society? First, the future kingdom promises a greater hope than the one that the marxist cherishes. It promises freedom and deliverance not just for the last generations who live after the revolution and enjoy its fruits at the cost of the suffering of others, but for all those who have lived in love and trustful dependence on God; for the kingdom promises resurrection. It promises a freedom that is total. The kingdom does not just bring an end to political oppression — though it promises a judgement and due reward to oppressors that even the Marxist cannot be certain of; it also brings freedom from the oppression of disease, of injustice, and of selfishness. It opens up a society where all serve each other in love for Christ.

This is not pie in the sky when you die. For the kingdom that is future criticizes every human ordering of society. Since no order on this earth can fully accommodate the kingdom of God, the kingdom acts as a continual critical agent, even after the revolution. Marxism makes the perfect world co-extensive with the great proletarian revolution, and has no tools for criticizing its own performance once the revolution is past. The whole world must in fact be remade to express the total kingdom of God; there must be a worldwide judgement, resurrection, a new creation. Jesus must return.

Because the kingdom will certainly come, and has already invaded there is a great motivation for change. Those who are members of the kingdom by God's grace must demonstrate the life of the kingdom in this world. They are promised that the powers of the kingdom are let loose in this world on their behalf. We are not wedded to a conservative position that gloomily says we must make the best of a bad job. The kingdom gives a group of people the new life of the kingdom — it produces the 'new man' that will readily and willingly live a life that shares with others, that is unselfish, that cares.

Those who enter the kingdom are to express its life in new structures. The reality of their membership is to be shown by the commitments to living the lifestyle of the kingdom, first of all in the new structure of the church. God's unique social and political programme was to create amidst all the structures and parties of Jewish politics, a new structure, the Christian church. In this structure men were to experience and live out a new way of being human beings in social relation to each other. The creation of a new structure on its own wouldn't solve the alienation that Peter would have felt for Matthew the tax-collector or for Mary Magdalen the prostitute. But once they were committed followers of Jesus, and members of the kingdom with God's spirit in their lives, they could not continue to relate to each other as Jew to tax-collector, or respectable Jewish male to harlot. They could not express their membership of God's kingdom as violent Zealots, or separatist Pharisees — Jesus created a new structure where the life of the kingdom was displayed.

In describing the life of this new community Jesus saw it as one where domination as a form of leadership would be out[28] — and where wealth would be shared. Jesus told the rich young ruler to sell his possessions and give to the poor, because Jesus' consistent teaching was that wealth is one of the greatest dangers to the spiritual life. Wealth can be like a camel in a doorway, blocking the entrance to the kingdom. Jesus did not tell the rich young man to have a detached attitude to his wealth. He is not satisfied that his followers should have a detached attitude to luxuries whereby they wouldn't feel suicidal if they lost their weekend cottages and hi-fi systems. Inward attitude must be matched by outward behaviour. If we are really going to demonstrate a detached attitude, Jesus would have us detach some wealth literally.

Jesus cursed the rich, the well fed and the satisfied. He described a rich fool who kept all his (honestly earned) goods to himself instead of distributing to the poor. He told the story of Dives who ignored the demands of charity and retained his wealth. Whenever the rich became disciples in the gospels they voluntarily parted with their possessions, like Zacchaeus and the wealthy converts in Acts.

Jesus did not advocate the possession-free life; but the total investment of life in the kingdom. Investing in wealth diverts us from investing treasure in heaven. The wealthy come under suspicion in the gospels because they are so bound by wealth that they are blind to the needs of the poor. Some are rescued with great difficulty — and prove the reality of their rescue by parting with their goods.

Andrew Kirk notes some anticipation of Marxist theory of James's warning to the rich: 'The warning of judgement upon the rich in James 5:1–6 contains elements which prefigure Marx's theory of surplus value, especially accumulated wealth and unjust profit ... James believes by his undifferentiated references to all rich (cf James 1:10–11) and (James 2:6; 4. 13,16) that differentiating riches are the clear result of exploitation (vv 4–6). This prophecy of doom against accumulated wealth is no less forceful than Marx's prophecy of the inevitable fall of capitalism.'[29]

It is not enough to say that these new structures that mirror a new attitude to men and wealth apply only to the church. Once men learn in the church the new relationships that are God's will for men, then they should seek to spread these expressions of God's love to the whole of society. For God is Lord of society, and the kingdom expresses the values he has for the creation of which he is Lord. The kingdom is redeemed creation. God's lordship for the whole of his creation is expressed *not* by a lower set of values and laws for unredeemed creation, but by expressing the values and standards of God's redeemed creation which is breaking in.

In practice it was in the church in the first century that men discovered that the new relationships in Christ were incompatible with the full rigours of slavery. In time Christian men, out of love for their neighbours worked to abolish slavery as a structure in society.

To the extent that some political systems and economic structures more faithfully represent human values as shown in Jesus' teaching, Christians should seek to implement those as far as possible in society. Where their political ability to do that is limited, they can still mourn over and dissociate from the rebellions systems that prevail. If Marxism more faithfully represents the truth of the economic situation and of the concerns of the Christian gospel than other possible systems, then Christians have a God-given duty to take it seriously, discuss with marxists, and together with them move beyond Marxism.

The following books and articles have been of especial help.

Jose Miguez Bonino   *Revolutionary Theology Comes of Age* (SPCK 1975)

Jose Miguez Bonino   *Christians and Marxists* (Hodder and Stoughton 1976)

Gustavo Guttierez   *A Theology of Liberation* (SCM 1974)

Peter Davids   'The poor man's gospel' *Themelios* (Spring 1976)

Donald Hay   *A Christian Critique of Capitalism* (Grove Books 1975)

Andrew Kirk   'The meaning of man in the debate between Christianity and Marxism' *Themelios* (Spring and Summer 1976)

Andrew Kirk   'Beyond Capitalism and Marxism: Dialogue with a Dialogue' *Latin American Theological Fraternity Bulletin 1976* (No 1,2)

John Stott   Review of Guttierez — 'Theology of Liberation' *Christian Leaders in Student Situations*, May 1975 (Available from UCCF, 38 De Montfort Street, Leicester)

John Yoder   *The Politics of Jesus* (Eerdmans 1972)

6

Evaluating Marxism: Some Christian Reflections[1]

DAVID LYON

Christian attitudes towards Marx and Marxism vary dramati-
cally. The perspective of the Soviet believer, working out his
years in a labour camp for the crime of teaching his children
from the Bible is vastly different from the perspective of the
Argentinian Christian who may see in Marxism an understanding of the social injustices of his country, and the
possibility of their removal. The Western college student,
moreover, might have yet another viewpoint on Marxism,
seeing it as a mode of interpretation in history or sociology
which appears to do justice to the evidence. So it is that we
find profound hatred and opposition, urgent and heartfelt
acceptance, and modest appreciation of Marxism as a valid
intellectual option all posing as 'Christian' attitudes towards
Marx and his ideas. Our aim is to find a biblically rooted
perspective on Marx and Marxism, one which is sensitive to
different situational contexts.

Much has been made of the so-called Christian-Marxist
dialogue, and it is in this interchange that there is perhaps

more fuzziness and confusion than in any other aspect of the relationship between Christians and Marxists. Roger Garaudy, a leading initiator of dialogue, has written of the shift from 'anathema to dialogue' (1967). But one sociologist has noted (MacIntyre 1969) that there has been a high cost involved in the achievement of this dialogue, as each 'side' seems to have been willing to accept a caricature of their position as a fair representation of what they claim to stand for. In other words, as the Christian minimizes the character of God and the fallenness of man, and the Marxist minimizes the need for revolution and the eventual abolition of religion, so each is forsaking what others would consider essential elements of their belief for the purpose of conversation. We shall do our best to avoid this here. Our purpose is not so much dialogue as the appreciation of Marx and Marxism from a Christian perspective. To appreciate something is to evaluate it justly, and so we need neither be wholly positive nor wholly negative. But for a just appreciation to be made, nothing of importance to the discussion must remain hidden.

To keep the discussion within manageable proportions, and yet to provide a useful starting point, we shall focus on 'man' and 'praxis' in the first instance. They are, in a sense, concepts common to both Christianity and Marxism, and provide helpful routes to the core of each way. While the question of 'who is man?' is as crucial as the question of 'who is God?', in the Christian way (and man, indeed, is only rightly understood in relation to God), in neither may the question be adequately answered in the abstract. The issues of practical activity, of living and of being, and uniting what is often called 'theory and practice', constitute part of the answer to 'who is man?'. Many Marxists have used the term 'praxis' (derived from Marx) to encapsulate this ideas/action combination. We shall look at these questions when we have established our general orientation.

But what is to comprise the basis of our 'Christian perspective'? How is this to differ from others which, though they claim to be 'Christian', are plainly contradictory? Granted, this is not an easy task, nor need we to expect it to be such. However, Christians are obliged to draw upon their Bibles (coupled with the illumination given by the Holy

Spirit) in the formation of their perspective, and so it is with the Bible that we begin. What follows is not an approach which is limited to Marxism, but rather one which may be fruitfully used in the appreciation of any way which men and women follow. It is deeply rooted in the whole Bible, both the Old and the New Testaments. I am calling it the 'Suppression and Substitution' approach.

The 'Suppression and Substitution' Approach

We shall first examine the biblicity of this perspective and then see how it may be used. What we mean by it is this: a non-Christian world-view and action-programme may be viewed simultaneously in two ways. Just as someone with only one eye cannot hope to have full vision, so it is that to see another way from only one of these viewpoints is to fail to understand it. As both eyes are necessary to complete vision, so it is necessary to think in terms both of suppression and substitution for the appreciation of other ways. In the case of Marxism, the Christian who sees it only as a heresy ('suppression') may believe that it may, with qualification, be married to Christian commitment; that it does not constitute a crucial threat to the Christian position. The Christian who sees Marxism only as an alternative religion, a substitute for the real thing, may only be diametrically opposed to it, seeing in it no good.

The approach is clearly present in the writings of Paul. Describing the fundamental state of mankind before God his Maker, he makes two points about our deviation from and forsaking of God's way. On the one hand, men 'suppress the truth in unrighteousness', and on the other they 'exchange the truth of God for a lie' (Romans 1:18 and 25). But these are dual processes, describing a situation in a complementary way. It is Paul, again, who applies this teaching when writing to the renegade faction in Galatia. Elements within the church were in trouble, and Paul explains why:

> I am amazed that you are so quickly deserting him who called you by the grace of Christ, for a *different* gospel; which is really not another; only there are some who are disturbing you, and

want to *distort* the gospel of Christ (Galatians 1: 6 and 7; my emphasis).

The issue involved is relevant to our later discussion of praxis, which warrants our considering it here. Specifically, ritual conditions were being imposed on the Galatian Christians; although appropriate in the Old Testament, these had no rightful place in the church of Christ. Before Christians might be accepted as full members of the worshipping community, they were required, even if they did not originate in a Jewish family, to abide by some Jewish laws. Paul responded firmly:

> Now that no-one is justified by the law before God is evident; for, 'The righteous man shall live by faith'. However, that Law is not a faith; on the contrary, 'He who practises them shall live by them' (Galatians 3:11,12).

The element of distortion (or suppression) here appears in the undue weight attached by the Galatians to law. However, it would be wrong to conclude that law no longer had any place in Christian teaching. The distortion needed to be corrected. Heresy was being promulgated; but as is the case with all heresy, it was *suppressed* or distorted truth. On the other hand, quite clearly, some people were making law the be-all and end-all of faith, and were insisting that without keeping the letter of the law salvation was impossible. To proclaim this was tantamount to proclaiming another religion, a *substitution* of true faith by a surrogate. For (as Paul insisted) no-one is justified by the law before God. It is as straightforward as that.

So we return to our perspective: that other ways (and we are talking specifically about the Marxist way) apart from Christianity may be considered both as suppression of or substitution for Christian commitment. Thus these other ways may include moments of truth, and close resemblances to Christian practice. They may be so taken out of context that in practice they are *untrue*, but this does not mean it is impossible that a non-Christian way might yet remind us of Christian truth.

It is to be hoped that this attitude will inform our overall appreciation of Marx and Marxism, so that we know better how far our positive agreement may go, and at what point we must be very careful. But even then, there will be tension; we dare not suggest neat categories into which Marxian notions will slot, allowing us the relief of relaxation. We mentioned that the Galatian example is appropriate to the latter discussion. This is partly so because the tension is illustrated in that early church situation. Faith is never thought of as something in the area of mere theory or abstract feelings. The biblical notion of faith is intensely practical, working itself out in everyday life obedience. In our day, no less than in New Testament times, Christians are constantly in danger of slipping into suppression and substitution. The kinds of issues with which we are engaged are of perennial importance, and will not be simply solved like an equation in mathematics. It is to be hoped, however, that although we may not discover any 'easy answers', we shall at least be able to see more clearly where we are going as we attempt to find a Christian perspective on Marxism.

Marx on Man

The main focus of the so-called Christian-Marxist dialogue has been the question of man: what *is* human? (Banks 1974a). Some have felt that Marx's view of man is a mere caricature of the Christian, whereas others believe the two views are so close that Marxism is the only worthy successor to Christianity as an interpreter of human existence (MacIntyre 1969). Some Marxists have suggested that the Christian view is mere idealism, viewing man *primarily* as a 'soul' or whatever. Insofar as non-Christian anthropologies (such as Platonism) have been superimposed on the Christian, Christians may agree (Miguéz-Bonino 1976:87). Let us first try to understand Marx's views, and then evaluate them in a Christian way.

Marx's man may not be put into a neat, static compartment, clinically isolated for scrutiny. 'Man is not an abstract being squatting outside the world,' he wrote; 'all history is nothing but a continual transformation of human nature'. Man is seen as continually recreating himself, developing progressively

in history. How does he develop? Through work. Marx
believed that work is the distinguishing characteristic of
mankind, as opposed to the animal kingdom. This is our
'species-being' as humans. Man is limited by nature, dependent on nature, but also capable of transforming nature to his
own ends.

How does man transform nature? For Marx, as a child of the
nineteenth century, the applied science of technology, which
is manifest above all in the machine, is *the means* which gives
man unprecedented power over nature. But, and here is the
rub, technology has also given man unprecedented power
over his fellows — because of the way in which industry is
organized under capitalism. The result is that man, whose
huge potential should make him the sun around which man
revolves, has become alienated.

Alienation, according to Marx, is the curse of industrial
civilization, in several ways. What the worker produces
becomes an alien object, owned by someone else, which
threatens him. He is estranged from his work, and thus from
himself — for his humanity (species-being) consists in free,
conscious, creative activity. And this estrangement expresses
itself socially as well, for he is estranged from his fellows.
Those owning the means of production are seen in opposition to those who are property-less, with only their labour-
power to sell, and the class struggle becomes a reality.

There is debate as to whether Marx was ultimately an
individualist or a collectivist (Banks 1974b:147) but whatever
the case, he saw social life as being intrinsic to man: 'The
essence of man is not an abstraction inherent in each
particular individual. The real nature of man is the totality of
social relations'. (Marx 1845:) So that when the 'totality of
social relations' is fragmented by antagonism of worker to
capitalist, man cannot be human. A revolutionary overthrow
of the capitalist system of production/exploitation becomes
necessary. It *will* come, not only because of the proletariat-
capitalist clash, but also because of the dialectical pattern of
history, and the destructive contradiction within capitalism
itself.[2] Revolution will end alienation and restore the possibility of the free development of all. Man will be free to be
himself again.

That, in a nutshell, is the essence of Marx's view. A major problem now faces us. In spelling out his view of humanity and history, Marx came embarrassingly close to a Christian understanding. To focus on a non-abstract, self-conscious person who finds intrinsic satisfaction in work and fulfilment only in the society of others, is to come very close to a biblical picture. For nowhere in Scripture are we given a 'list of components' view of the person of man — the fundamental things we know concern the 'image of God' and 'fallenness'. We also know of salvation in and through the God-man Jesus Christ. But one does not have to look far to see that *sociality* and *work* are intrinsic aspects of the created life of mankind as well. If we confine ourselves only to the Genesis account, we see that man is intrinsically social, being made male-and-female. Solitariness is shown as an undesirable state of affairs, since it is 'not good for man to be alone'. Moreover, people were also clearly made for fellowship with God as well as each other, which is another hint of our intrinsic sociality. But people were also made to work. That, too, is part of what it is to be human. All manner of work, including manual labour in the field, mental labour of animal-classification, emotional work of child-rearing, and economic work of being caretakers, or stewards of the earth — all these and others were given to man *before* the fall. And when the fall came, both human sociality and work relationships were disrupted by that fundamental rebellious split from God. Judging from the experience of Adam and Eve, and of Cain and Abel, fallenness has to do with exploitation, treating people as objects, and 'means' and jealousy related to the production of different goods. Such common situations in the modern industrial world, were already wreaking havoc 'East of Eden'. And the burning social criticism of the Old Testament prophets is testimony enough to the fact that what began at the fall, and is with us today, was also just as prevalent in that Eastern agricultural economy.

So what can we say? How may we meaningfully distinguish between 'suppression' and 'substitution' in Marx, and how necessary is the attempt? We must say, at the outset, that Marx rejected religion as such, and Christianity in particular. He was an atheist, and his atheism plus his belief that man needs no religious reference-point other than himself, is the reason why it is necessary to criticise his ideas (although several participants in the 'dialogue' discounted the importance of his atheism.) Those beliefs have far-reaching implications in the social and political realm. Marx said that 'the critique of religion ends in the teaching that man is the supreme being for man' (Marx 1846). And as one Marxist has clearly put it: 'If Marx's whole project is to help revolutionise the social world with the effect of having people act in accordance with laws we produce from ourselves, then, from this point of view, the whole project makes sense only from the premise of atheism' (Schuller 1975: 337).

If man is all there is, then man is answerable only to himself. Human autonomy (that is, personally governing the direction of one's own life, without reference to God) becomes the goal and the norm. And yet, attempted human autonomy is precisely that which, in the biblical view, is equivalent to man's fallenness, not to the image of God. So it is in this 'post-Christian humanism', as Zylstra (1974) has called it, that we find the root of the antagonism between Christianity and Marxism. For the substitution that has taken place is for man to replace God as the arbiter, the law-giver, the creator. In Marx, man alone creates himself, legislates by means of human reason, and decides how best he may pursue his own goals. His inability to do so is seen as pathological. In Scripture, by contrast, God created man to be answerable to him, and ordains the basic structures of free human existence out of a concern for the welfare of his creatures and his own glory. Thus it is the attempt to find autonomy, rather than its lack, which is seen as pathological in this view. Here is the substitution: there is a complete antithesis between worshipping the creature, on the one hand, and the Creator, on the other.

We need to remember at this point that the notion of fallenness, so crucial to the Christian position, is very often underplayed by Christians wishing to engage in the 'dialogue'. Hardly surprising, then, that the notion of substitution is also under-emphasized; yet it is this very factor of man's fallenness that explains why, despite revolutions in Marx's name which have purported to end alienation, there is little evidence of 'content' or the 'free development of all' in aspiring-to-be-socialist countries. For the Christian, while realizing that some social environments *are* more conducive to right living than others, continues to believe that no number of new environments can change the heart of man. Of course, 'dialogue' contributors such as Moltmann (1968), following Schaff and Kolakowski, recognize that ending slavery only *reduces misery*, it does not make men happy. And as Ton (1976) has shown, it certainly does not produce 'new men'. But this kind of caution does not stop oppressed people pinning their hopes on Marxism in a messianic way. After all, the Marxist gospel *is* very attractive as an explanation and a programme to deal with the evil world of ruthless capitalism. But its appeal is also its danger; it is a *total* appeal, which turns a blind eye to the limitations of the liberation in order to maintain popular credibility.

So much for the element of *substitution*. We must now turn to that of *suppression*. This is where we see how close Marx came to Christian understanding, and also how he reminds Christians of their *task*. More than one commentator has observed that, if nineteenth-century Christians had been faithful to the biblical witness, in exposing evil in its cosmic and social dimensions, Marx would have been redundant. He rightly saw that evil forces are at work in capitalist-industrial civilization; that the worlds men make tend to be inhuman and unjust for some. But what is missing from his work is the notion of sin: here is the element of suppression. Although his was a radical analysis of an evil world, it was not radical enough (Goudzwaard 1972, 1979). For it is clear that Marx opposed many social institutions that Christians ought to oppose, and recognized dimensions of human life in which Christians have the duty to act. It has taken until the 1970s for Christians to engage in a serious critique of capitalism from evangelical perspectives (e.g., Hay, 1974, Goudzwaard 1972). Until recently, certain pressures (for example, of big business establishment connection with the church) have been strongly in favour of a Christianity-capitalism association, as an unquestionable social arrangement. The very notion that there *can be* a Christian understanding of social life (which goes beyond discussion of marriage and the family) or a

Christian understanding of economic life (which goes beyond 'if a man will not work, let him not eat') is one which is only slowly penetrating our complacently individualistic and pietistic Christian circles.

Yes, Marx speaks to Christians. He has raised the challenge of economic and social life in an age of industrial capitalism, starkly and without compromise. But Marxism is a suppression, a distortion of Christian truth, even when it highlights the weaknesses of our social witness. To take but one example, Marx (himself bourgeois) tries to see the world through the eyes of a proletarian. All situations are seen as examples of oppression, false consciousness, alienation and exploitation in which the capitalists, having outgrown their useful phase of introducing that vital technology, are cast as the maintainers of evil social structures. The cause of liberating the workers is the only important one: their interests are paramount. This is not a Christian analysis. For while the biblical understanding would expose oppression and greed, it is not the interests of one group that are made supreme, but the demands of God on *all* involved. And the sympathy and compassion of Christ, though he certainly preached 'a poor man's gospel' (Davids 1976), were for the rich and defrauding tax-collectors as well as the destitute. We shall see more of this suppression aspect as we now consider 'praxis'.

Marx on Praxis

'*Social life is essentially* practical. All mysteries which mislead theory into mysticism find their rational solution in human practice and in the comprehension of this practice' (Marx 1845).

Marx, with other radical Hegelians in the 1840s, got very excited about the idea of *praxis*. It led him to state that while previous philosophers had only *interpreted* the world, the real point was to *change* it. Philosophy, thought of as praxis, was to be concerned with practical activity, not theoretical abstraction, being neither mere 'theory', nor mere 'practice', but a unique combination of the two. Its thrust is opposed both to thoughtless *activism* and to impractical *philosophizing*. In praxis, experience is the source of theory, which informs action. Ideas are inseparable from activity, and they have meaning only in relation to each other.

The extent to which this notion is *substitution* for an aspect of Christian life must be immediately evident from the Marx quotation: '*All* mysteries ... find their solution in human practice ...' Mysticism, in which Marx included Christianity, was a sidetrack from practice which is where mysteries are solved. The contradiction is apparent. For Christianity, Jesus Christ is *the* way, truth and life — *only* in relation to him are mysteries solved, evil overcome and sins forgiven. This is another place where Marx is rejecting the faith of the Bible. Praxis, for him, is an alternative to Christian (or any other formally religious) commitment. He has 'exchanged the truth of God for a lie' (Romans 1:25).

But I wish to draw attention to the more *suppressive* implications of praxis. Jose Miguéz-Bonino (1976), an Argentinian theologian, more than any other writer in the Christian-Marxist encounter, has suggested that praxis is an aspect of Christian commitment. The classic text, if one is required, is Jeremiah 22:16: Josiah 'judged the cause of the poor and needy; then it was well. Is this not to know me, says the Lord?' Or Christ himself: '...everyone who hears these words of mine, and *acts upon them*, may be compared to a wise man...' (Matt. 7:24). The unity of 'theory and practice' or 'doctrine and life-style' is intrinsic to Christinianity. It was often said of new Christians, not only that they had been 'saved' (which is what God had done), but also that they were 'obedient to the faith' (Acts 6:7). No wonder that James could write that 'faith without works is dead' (James 2:26)! Yet Evangelicals have been guilty of making a split precisely here. 'Only believe!' has been the word from the pulpit, as if intellectual assent to a bunch of propositions is the sum of Christianity. We forget, at our peril, that when Christians were *given* that nickname, there is little doubt that it was not on the grounds of *theological* orthodoxy with regard to Christ's teachings. It was because they *practised the truth* that they were called Christians.

Miguéz stresses the concrete obedience which the biblical writers identify with 'knowing God' — there being no *separate* moment of knowing God *prior* to obedience. He

argues that Christians have lost this unity whenever they use
phrases like 'knowing God *and* walking in his ways.' To know
God *is* to walk in his ways. Thus we might suggest that the
Christian equivalent of praxis is knowing God. For knowing
God involves knowing things about God which are worked
out in practical, everyday life. To know God is to have a
personal relationship with him and to live the life that he
requires and desires (Packer 1973, especially chapters 1 and
2). As Miguéz reminds us, this is frequently bound up with
pursuing justice, righteousness and equity in the social
world. And these facets of Christian witness are almost as
frequently overlooked.

But we must go on to ask the question as to *how* the Marxian
notion of praxis is a distortion or 'suppression' of the notion
of knowing God? The very terms yield the clue. Praxis has no
referent but man. Praxis is the activity of would-be autonomous man. Knowing God has a personal referent: it is a
relationship with our Maker. Girardi (1969), a Roman Catholic contributor to the dialogue, reminds us that praxis
involves evidence of success, historical verification if you
like, and also an ideal, or goal. Focusing on the latter, Girardi
ends by contrasting what he sees as Marx's goal of 'collective
freedom' with his 'Christian' ideal of personal freedom. He
has not transcended the personal/social dichotomy, which
indicates an either/or position. So Marxism, being collectivist, is 'not humanistic enough'. Another problem with
Girardi is that he soft-pedals on the relationship between
'freedom' and 'fallenness'. In the Christian understanding, it
is our fallenness which renders us unfree.

In relation to God, however, there need not be an either/or
split between the personal and the social. I want to say that
knowing God (which Miguéz thinks of as Christian praxis) is
fundamentally personal, but yet copes uniquely with the
problem of fallenness, personally and socially. (It is difficult
to express this firmly enough, but as I pointed out earlier, as
persons we are *intrinsically* social.) For to know God is to come
to him, in Christ, (the Word made flesh), and to be in a
peaceful, non-estranged relationship with him. If the essence
of fallenness is rebellion against, or estrangement from God,
then the essence of knowing God is living freely before him,

with a conscience cleansed by the blood of Christ. And this is Christian freedom.

But it is clear from biblical material that sin has deep-seated *social* manifestations also: people and generations are described variously as stiff-necked, crooked, and perverse. And Christians should aim at following Christ himself, as he proclaimed the jubilee (Luke 4:18) — including 'freedom to the downtrodden'. But this liberty, or freedom *from* oppression, is not to be confused with Christian freedom itself. Nevertheless, Scripture is eloquent on the matter of liberty, which is assumed in the biblical treatment of justice and equity.

Knowing God relates to *God's* righteousness and so on (as opposed to justice for the proletariat *only*). But it is a relationship which copes with the *continuing* and *universal* *effects* of fallenness. For knowing God is a *process*, described biblically as 'sanctification', whereby Christians, living freely before God, aim increasingly at realising the Christ-like life in a hostile and alien world. It can cope with political decisions — which may be eschewed as 'compromise' by Marxists — but which involve 'lesser evil' choices. These may be 'right' before God. Even Christian freedom, given the continuing effects of fallenness, may be misused, but the ideal of Christian praxis, or knowing God, is clear: 'For you were called to freedom, brethren; only do not turn your freedom into an opportunity for the flesh, but through love serve one another' (Galatians 5:13).

Where have we come?

We shall try to summarize the main burden of our discussion, and apply the principles gleaned to the specific problems, to which we alluded at the outset.

Marx, in his understanding of man, reminds Christians of some important matters, albeit in a distorted way. The centrality of satisfying work (reflecting the character of God as his image), and sociality as inherent in the human person (but sociality with *God*, as well as fellow-humans); these are two examples. But Marx's man attempts autonomy, and in so doing reveals what, in the biblical view, is his fallenness.

Here is the substitution: man, rather than God, is the reference point, the arbiter of right and wrong, and at this point Marxism cannot but be seen as an alternative religion.

Other crucial aspects of Christian commitment are raised by 'praxis'. We suggest that this is the Marxian distortion or suppression of knowing God, and insofar as it is *the* criterion of truth, it is a substitution as well. But the contradictions within Marx's work have necessitated interpretations: we now have to contend with Engels', Lenin's, and Mao's versions — to name but three. With them in particular, revolution became *the praxis* par exellence. And for them, Marx's humanism is eclipsed by the necessity to make revolution, whatever the cost. Although we have not touched on this issue, we could say that Marx cannot stand alone. His work *must* be interpreted in some way. Within the basic boundaries of post-Christian humanism, praxis ends with anarchy or authoritarianism. So that while praxis may remind Christians of a long-forgotten aspect of commitment, on its own it is insufficient. Xenia Howard-Johnson is right to remind us that a kind of Marxian praxis has led to terror and oppression. So of Miguéz-Bonino, she says he has 'established that there are circumstances in which Christians and Marxists can and no doubt should work together, but when the Marxists in question are also Leninists this is no longer possible without gross distortion or self-deception.' (1976:3)

So, does the suppression-substitution analysis work? Is it helpful to see Marxism as both suppression and substitution? With regard to Christians in socialist countries, the most common activity has been trying to maintain constitutional rights of religious groups to practise their faith. Many have seen clearly that Marxist Leninism is a demand for heart-allegiance, which is not satisfied until the confession is made 'the state (or the people) is Lord'. Ton's strategy, as a Baptist in Romania, has been to try to unmask the religious substitution component (by showing that ultimately Marxist-Leninism cannot 'produce the goods' of new men), and to agree as far as possible to work within the socialist state as a Christian citizen. He is saying that as far as justice and equity are concerned, he is willing to work alongside Marxists —

even though the basis of their 'justice' is a distortion of biblical standards.

What of Christians who are in the midst of revolutionary ferment? I suggest that, especially if they are in South America, they are more likely to forget the *substitution* aspect than the distortion. Miguéz-Bonino, calling Marxism a 'project' (which is similar to Garaudy's 'methodology') suggests that for the 'greater good', Christians may join with Marxists in strategic alliance. He asserts this, even though he recognizes that Marxists see Marxism as *more* than a 'project', and make totality-claims on its behalf. The dangers are obvious. But it is easy to criticize South American Christians from the sidelines, and in limited local situations, Miguéz Bonino may be right.[3] One imagines, however, that Christians would have to make their position *very* clear, and once that has been done, one wonders how many Marxists would in fact join hands with them.

This relates to another group I mentioned: Christians in student situations. Here again, it is vital to maintain the suppression-substitution distinction. Jacques Ellul, the Bordeaux sociologist, has referred to Marxism as a 'way of seeing', quite compatible in many respects, with (his) Christian commitment (Holloway 1970:5). As a contribution to social interpretation, Marxism is difficult to avoid in the contemporary university — in most countries. And it can not be denied that Marxist scholarship has sharpened the critical edge of several disciplines, especially history, economics, political science and sociology (although the internal contradictions of Marxism remain). But again, it is all too easy for Christians, seeing a shadow of their faith in Marxism, to mistake the shadow for the reality, and to follow that. But until Christian social-theology gets to grips with the burning issues of the late twentieth century, from a thoroughgoing biblical perspective, the shadow will continue to have more substance than the reality. If the suppression-substitution perspective is true to the biblical outlook, then it is a matter of sheer hard work, in the power of the Holy Spirit, for Christian students to work out what is distortion and what substitution, and how far each affects social interpretation. Both uncritical acceptance and outright rejection are inadequate responses.

One other word of warning. There is often a temptation, when faced with a 'challenge' to Christian commitment, to try to counter it on its own terms; in this case, to try to 'match Marx' with a better alternative at each of *his* points. But this can be misleading. We must not do what some dialogue-contributors have done: forget what is distinctive about Christian commitment. Andrew Kirk (himself a member of the Argentinian scene) suggests that in '*biblical* realism' there is an authentic Christian reply to the challenge of Marxism. He has shown (1976:92–3) that biblical realism is both a destroyer of idols (which I suggest can include Marxism as well as capitalism) and a proposer of its own socio-political programme. In the latter he includes the establishment of justice, solidarity with the oppressed, following the New Testament pattern for the church-community, and applying a de-ideologized gospel in academic work.

The obvious difficulty which arises here is that few of us have the direct opportunity to 'establish justice' or demonstrate 'solidarity'. It is my conviction that there are a variety of callings in this sphere, and while *all* can be aware of the issues, very few will be involved in an immediate or deep way. But there is much in ordinary, everyday life which needs to be confronted with 'biblical realism'. We dare not allow Marx to divert our attention from applying our faith to that which may seem mundane after class-struggle and revolution: compassionate neighbourliness, loving and disciplined family relationships, and critical conscientiousness in daily work.

Where do we go from here?

Having said that Christians should not attempt to counter Marxism on its terms, we need finally to be reminded of the uniqueness of the Christian gospel, centring as it does in a person: Jesus Christ. Although, as Kirk suggests, there are guidelines in the Bible which relate to socio-political programmes, these are only part of the total Christian world-view and way of life. Marxism inflates a socio-political programme into a total world-view and way of life, claiming that there is nothing else. Marx knew nothing of that radical end to the deepest human alienation, between man and God, in the surprise and disarming tactic of the death of Christ. Marx knew nothing of an ethic based on the 'last things', which have as their focus the return of the same Jesus Christ. (Travis (1976) takes up some of these themes in an engaging and relevant way in *The Jesus Hope*.) In the last analysis, however much we may thank Marx for confronting us with his picture of the of the stark realities of exploitation and inhumanity in industrial-capitalist society, we will not heed the beckoning finger of Marx, but Jesus, when he says 'follow me'. But let us consider, lastly, how this might work itself out in terms of the 'variety of callings' which we mentioned above.

We have already suggested that slightly different responses to Marx may be appropriate with different situations: Latin America, Eastern Europe, Africa, China, or universities anywhere. But that is only a difference of emphasis; the biblical method remains the same. And that biblical method also reveals the necessity of seeing different *callings* in the world. Not all are called to be political leaders, like Daniel, Moses, and Joseph. In fact, this is more likely to be the exception rather than the rule. But that does not exempt the majority. There is another way. I wish to indicate that Christians may be called to social-political involvement in (at least) two ways, which may complement each other. These ways relate to what Jesus said in the sermon on the mount, about our being the salt of the earth, and the city on a hill (Matt.5:13–16).

Salt

This, which is probably the more common understanding of the Christian presence in the world, has to do with *influence through contact*. The salt must flavour the earth through shoulder-rubbing contact with it; Christians act as preservative grains, preventing social decay. It is the position put forward, for example, by Sir Frederick Catherwood in Britain, when he speaks of reforming society according to God's law (Catherwood 1964, 1975). The idea is that, via the 'system', one uses a position in a political party, a pressure group, a journalistic position, and so on, to reform things in line with

God's demands. This is part of the (traditionally Reformed) vision of Christianizing society. In Britain, this tradition has boasted men like Wilberforce and Shaftesbury, each of whom fought injustices associated with imperialism and industrial capitalism because of their Christian convictions. They did so through parliamentary action in what today might be scorned as a 'paternalistic' attitude, but which, properly interpreted, has biblical precedents.

So this is certainly a Christian calling, which applies to *all* believers. And it is one to be taken very seriously at every point where we have direct contact with the 'system'. But we may be more or less effective, depending on the extent of our influence. Knowing of those who can use their position to promote right living, and to oppose oppression and injustice can produce more than one effect. It can make Christians more prayerful, and supportive of those who are in more obviously salting positions. This is good. But it can also lead to a feeling of apathy and complacency, because it is felt that the presence of the minority in the public sphere exonerates others from participation. But Jesus did not only say we are the salt of the earth; we are also a city set on a hill: a light which cannot be hidden.

City

We could think of this aspect of Jesus' injunction as having to do with *example through contrast*. The city-community shows the surrounding peoples what God's kingdom looks like — as nearly as it can. It is an alternative reality, free to try out Christian ideas without waiting for changes in the 'system'. Augustine, though he combined the salt and city ideas, clearly envisaged a 'Christian city' of the church, living within an alien 'city of the world'. Francis Schaeffer, too, has hinted at this, by speaking of 'pilot plants of the kingdom'. This aspect of the Christian presence is associated with the (traditionally Anabaptist) belief in the 'otherness' of the people of God, as they provide a bright contrast to those enslaved by the system and by self-pleasing. Many young evangelicals in North America, disgusted with the churches' compliance with the evils of the dominant social forces in their affluent culture, have chosen rather to go this way. They wish to provide a biblical contrast, not only with an alien and God-ignoring state, but with what is scathingly termed 'civil religion'. One leading spokesman, Jim Wallis, has written:

> The church is called to relate to the world as a new community of people who are being transformed by Christ. This means that, first of all and at the basis of all that we do, we must seek to become a kingdom-conscious body of people who, by their very existence and presence, call into question the values, assumptions, and very structure of their world and free people to live in alternative ways. (1976:107)

This vision of what Christians are to be in the world is one with which everyday folk may more easily identify. We can all work at making our churches real communities of fellowship in a risen Lord, where pure biblical doctrines are not only preached but actively lived in neighbourhoods and cities. Christians can demonstrate the peacemaking power of the gospel, and the harmony that follows the breakdown of economic and social barriers in Christ (Galatians 3:28). As we have already suggested, it seems that the 'world-changing' challenge of Marxism can divert the energies of Christians into a futile chase after elusive new societies, when the biblical model for Christian activity is this ongoing alternative to the surrounding social patterns. The Bible tells us far more about being God's people here and now (and we have so much to learn!) than it does about social-political strategy at national and international levels.

Christians are *all* to be both salt *and* cities, but, interpreted in this way, it is clear that only a few are called to deep political involvement of the public kind, while all may take part in the alternative realities of the church-community and the Christian family. And the latter may ultimately be a deeper political threat to the established orders of power and domination than we at first imagine. The patterns for racial integration, understanding between employers and employees, simple, low-consumption lifestyles, and trothful families, unspoiled by sexism and arbitrary 'discipline' would emerge *from the church*. Who then would need Marxism?

To sum up. The old Christian-Marxist dialogue, in its late sixties form, is past its peak. But there are still Christians, and there are still Marxists, who must reckon with each other. This chapter is a call to Christian commitment, which justly evaluates Marx, and is manifest in biblically-realistic and situationally-sensitive action. We glanced in a cursory way at 'man' and 'praxis', trying to see them in the biblical perspective of suppression and substitution: they are key areas of debate. But the jolt that the notion of praxis gives to Christian complacency reminds us that mere debate is futile. We have to work out in practice, in our own situations, the implications of the marxist challenge, as we try to be the salt of the earth and cities set on hills, our hearts engaged with God's requirements for all people.

References

Banks, R.	1974a 'The Search for Man in Christian-Marxist Dialogue', *Theology*, 77, 137–147
Banks, R.	1974b 'Theology and Marxism: The Contribution of Emil Brunner and Reinhold Niebuhr', *Interchange*, 15:143–162
Bottomore, T.B. and Rubel, M.	1961 *Karl Marx: Selected Writings in Sociology and Social Philosophy*, Harmondsworth, Penguin
Catherwood, H.F.R.	1964 *The Christian in Industrial Society* London, Tyndale Press. 1975 *A Better Way*, London, Inter-Varsity Press
Davids, P.	1976 'The Poor Man's Gospel', *Themelios*, 1, 2, 37–41
Garaudy, R.	1967 *From Anathema to Dialogue: The Challenge of Christian-Marxist Co-operation*, London, Collins
Girardi, G.	1968 *Marxism and Christianity*, New York, MacMillan
Goudzwaard, B.	1972 *Economic Stewardship versus Capitalist Religion*, Toronto, Institute for Christian Studies (mimeo)

Goudzwaard, B.	1979 *Capitalism and Progress: A Diagnosis of Western Society*, Grand Rapids, Eerdmans
Hay, D.	1975 *A Christian Critique of Capitalism*, Nottingham, Grove
Holloway, J.	1970 *Introducing Jacques Ellul*, Grand Rapids, Eerdmans
Howard-Johnson	1976 Editorial, *Religion in Communist Lands*, 4, 2, 3
Kirk, A.	1976 'The Meaning of Man in the Debate Between Christianity and Marxism', p. 42 in *Themelios*, 1, 3
MacIntyre, A.	1968 *Marxism and Christianity*, Harmondsworth, Penguin
MacIntyre, A.	1969 'The Christian-Communist Rapprochement: Some Sociological Notes and Questions', in Martin, D. (ed) *Sociological Yearbook of Religion in England*, London, SCM
McLellan, D.	1975 *Marx*, London, Fontana
Marx, K.	1843 *Critique of Hegel's Philosophy of Right* (Bottomore & Rubel, 1961)
Marx, K.	1845 *Theses on Feuerbach* (in Bottomore and Rubel, 1961)
Marx, K.	1846 *The German Ideology* (in Bottomore and Rubel, 1961)
Miguéz-Bonino, J.	1976 *Christians and Marxists*, London, Hodder and Stoughton, and Eerdmans, Grand Rapids
Moltmann, J.	1968 'The Revolution of Freedom', in Ogletree, T.W. (1968)
Mouw, R.	1976 *Politics and the Biblical Drama*, Grand Rapids, Eerdmans
Ogletree, T.W.	1968 *Openings for Christian-Marxist Dialogue*, Nashville and New York, Abingdon
Schuller, P.M.	1975 'Karl Marx's Atheism', *Science and Society*, 39, 3, 331–344
Ton, J.	1976 'The Socialist Quest for the New Man', *Christianity Today*, March 26
Travis, S.	1974 *The Jesus Hope*, London, Word Books
Wallis, J.	1976 *Agenda for biblical people*, New York, Harper Row

Zylstra, B.

1974 'The Post-Christian Humanism of Karl Marx', *Reformasie en Revolusie*, Potchefstroom, Institute for the Advancement of Calvinism. A brief version published as 'Karl Marx: Radical Humanist', in *Vanguard*, December, 1973

7

The Alternative Radical

TONY PEARCE

I became disillusioned with bourgeois society when I was eight years old. I remember it very clearly. My father was promoted in his job and we moved from a village in Hertfordshire where I was happy with many friends to Bedford where I was unhappy and had no one to play with. Being fairly bright and my parents now having money to spare, I won a place at Bedford School, the local Public School with a history going back four hundred years. It was a great honour and achievement. I was discouraged however from playing with the children from the nearby council estate and I grew very lonely. Yet at school I received insults that my parents were nouveau riche and not on an equal social level. So at this early age I discovered the reality of class division. I did not like it. The success of my father together with my own success had meant unhappiness. I began therefore to equate success with unhappiness. Out of this experience was born the mood which dominated my adolescence — a deep-rooted rebellion against bourgeois society and all that represented it: parents, school and church.

'How beastly the bourgeois is', wrote D.H. Lawrence, and I agreed. Inwardly and, when I had the courage, outwardly, I raged against the hypocrisy of social gatherings where people were polite to one another's face, but tore each other apart

behind their backs; against the rat race and the all important
drive to accumulate wealth and prestige, which I could see
did not give real happiness to anyone; against an empty
religion where people prayed to God and asked for his will to
be done and then lived to please themselves; against the gulf
between the rich and the poor, and against the weapons of
destruction which threatened the very survival of humanity.
At the age of seventeen I had become an angry young man
who scorned religion, tradition and authority. A schoolboy
intellectual doing French, and German A-level, I was
attracted by the writings of Sartre, Camus, D.H. Lawrence,
Brecht and Rimbaud, by the songs of Bob Dylan and Joan
Baez, and by satirical magazines like *Private Eye*. I loved to
ridicule the Public School establishment and to deflate the
pretensions of those who thought they were superior to
others because of an accident of birth. I had an ally and a
comrade in an American Jew called Steve. I felt strongly about
the Jews, and particularly about protecting Steve when others
picked on him because of his Jewishness. I did not know why
this was, unless perhaps I sensed that they like me were
outsiders, alienated from bourgeois society, yet wiser and
deeper than the society which refused to accept them.

During my sixth form years two political events made me
aware of the big world outside. The first was the Cuban
missile crisis. I was terrified by the thought of being on the
brink of a Third World War. Furthermore it made life seem
futile. For what purpose had man struggled to create culture,
technology, political systems, religions, if everything could
be destroyed in one moment by a nuclear bomb? What was
the point of my own personal studies for university if one
bomb could wipe it out? At a deeper level, what do I live for if
the bombs don't fall and I live to be an old man of eighty? Was
not human existence some sick joke set in motion by a
presently indifferent Being?

The second experience was a trip to Berlin. I stood in the
Potzdamer Platz where once the fascist youth of the Third
Reich had roared out their idolatry of the monster Hitler, and I
saw the Wall snaking its way through the city. Ugly breeze
blocks fringed with barbed wire; soldiers with machine guns
watching from the Eastern side; slogans of contempt daubed

in paint on the Western side. The Berlin wall came to symbolise the human race for me: man divided against himself, manipulated by sinister forces he did not understand and condemned to an absurd existence from which there was no escape.

I went to East Berlin and met a man named Klaus. He asked me to visit his parents who lived in the West and to take his mother some flowers for her birthday. I agreed to do so and I found their flat in West Berlin, where I was greeted with great joy and kindness by the elderly couple who had not seen their son for three years. They were both deaf and dumb and we had to communicate by writing messages on paper. My heart went out to them. 'Were they born deaf and dumb', I thought, 'or had some shocking experience robbed them of the power of speech and hearing?' I felt torn inside by my own helplessness, not only in face of their handicap but in face of the walls of hatred which divided humanity. What force could rebuild bridges of love and understanding, and bring a new age of peace and humanity? Nothing I had seen in Christianity gave me any hope that that was the way. The churches I had been to simply observed a dead ritual week after week without any relevant message for modern man. Jesus I liked but not his church.

What about Communism? But the Communists had built the Berlin Wall. Communism had imposed itself on the German people through Soviet tanks and secret police. Its ideal however appealed to me very much. 'The philosophers have only interpreted the world. The point however is to change it'. I wanted a changed world, to end selfishness, corruption and war. 'From each according to his ability. To each according to his need'. 'Peace and Socialism' — nice slogans; was this the way?

The summer after leaving school, 1965, was spent in the freedom and excitement of travel. I joined the bands of restless young people from Europe and North America, hitchhiking across Europe, some setting their horizons upon the far East in their search for undertanding and fulfillment, the rest of us being content with the exotic beauty of a city like Istanbul, with its dirty streets and noisy bazaars. Istanbul influenced me for another reason. There I met a Turkish student who had gone to great lengths for me in trouble I was having there with the authorities. He could see that I loved Istanbul. He said, 'You like Istanbul? But you don't see it as it really is. It is a rotten, corrupt place. We want to change it.' I asked how, and he told me that he was a Communist. His communism was more than ideas. He said that the Turkish government was keen to repress all left wing activity in the country, but if necessary he would give his life for the communist cause. For the first time I was speaking to someone whose beliefs meant more to him than his own self-interest. It was an impression which stayed with me long after all the transitory impressions of the many cities I had visited that summer had faded.

One of my first friends at Cambridge was a communist. He was also a Jew. He introduced me to a meeting of the college communist party. It was a great disappointment. There were three people present, all talking in a language which I could not grasp. It was no less irrelevant than that which I had heard in church. My friend also disappointed me in time. He threw away his revolutionary identity and began to conform to bourgeois ways. I followed suit outwardly at least. But still inwardly I seethed with indignation at the petty minded class and intellectual snobbery of Cambridge and all the social climbing and hypocrisy I saw around me. I was still an outsider, and deeply unhappy. I threw myself into partying and drinking and boasting and in my final year withdrew completely to delve into books on philosophy and literature, seeking an answer to those fundamental questions which still obsessed me. I read the Greeks, Shakespeare, Goethe, Dostoevsky, Nietzsche, Kafka, Freud and Marx. I never considered the Bible; after all Nietzsche had said God was dead and I could see nothing contrary to that statement, though I needed to find a belief in someone greater than myself. 'They tell me God is dead, across the void I hear them say it. But tell me then, why, oh why in all this god-dying silence should we continue to exist?'

I left Cambridge with an upper second in English and a very confused and disorientated mind. I identified with characters like the hero of the film 'The Graduate', being myself 'a little worried about my future'. I had no direction or aim. A top job in commerce or industry was possibly open to me, as also a career in academic research but the idea of either revolted me. I wanted to cease from becoming a bourgeois intellectual in revolt against society and to become involved in the process towards a better world.

So I went to work for the Simon community in London. The community got its name from Simon of Cyrene who carried Jesus's cross but it was not a Christian organization. It accepted workers from all faiths and none and aimed at helping the homeless, the tramps, the meths drinkers, and the drug addicts who live in the streets and doss at night in derelict houses and under the bridges at Charing Cross and Waterloo. I enjoyed the work very much at first, especially the nights when we went out on a soup run, taking soup and food and clothing to the men sleeping out on the Thames Embankment. So strange that here, just down the road from the Central Offices of Government and of the massive multi-national companies, hundreds of derelict men and women existed from day to day in a hell of pain, rejection and futility. Once I got over my initial nervousness I found these people much easier to communicate with than straight respectable people. There was no need for them to cover up the reality of their lives and their failures. It was all too obvious.

After a week at the main house at Chalk Farm, they sent me to the 'Shelter', a decaying tenement building in Bethnal Green. My first encounter with the Shelter was a traumatic one. They had been drinking heavily when I arrived. One of the men, Walter, a Scot from Glasgow, took an instant dislike to me. 'I want ye oot', he started to bawl. He went on and on and the others started to join in. The man in charge, Gerry, a believing Irish Catholic, tried to calm them down. He then took me aside and told me not to take it personally. They were in a bad mood that day, he said. I was shaken. I had tried to help humanity and had been received with rejection and hostility. I wanted to run away but knew that I could not admit defeat so easily. Then I noticed a card pinned onto the wall with the prayer of St. Francis written on: 'Lord make me an instrument of thy peace'. The words were so beautiful and moved me in a strange way. How I wanted to be an instrument of peace and bring light and hope to a dark world! Yet not through God or through the Church. Hadn't the Church been anything but an instrument of peace through-out the centuries, bringing strife and oppression? And why should we turn to God for help? The religious crutch was for the weak and inadequate, for the time of man's ignorance. We had to believe in man and discover the resources within man himself that would transform the world from its present misery and futility and create a new world order.

Apart from Gerry, the rest of us in the community were young people without any religious belief, motivated by humanism and in some cases, by a revolutionary form of socialism. I soon overcame the difficult beginnings and settled in to the community life. I made a special friendship with a tramp called 'O.B'. He had done much of his begging in Cambridge and had a high regard for Cambridge students. How odd that the bourgeois education from which I was fleeing was the thing which linked me with this old tramp. But O.B. was a sick man, and everyone in the community knew that he was dying. One night he told me this himself. It cut me like a knife. What hope or comfort could I, an agnostic humanist, offer a man who had lived an awful life? A Mother Superior once asked me about O.B. and wondered if I had ever had a chance to talk to him about God? 'No', I said quickly. I wanted to reply that I was not working out of Christian charity, and that not only Christians cared about others. Her question angered and confused me. I thought: 'Suppose I did want to talk about God, what would I say?' I soon dismissed the idea from my mind. It was only the older generation which thought God relevant. Another ideology was drawing my generation — Marxism.

It was October 1968, the time of the great Vietnam demonstration in London. Under the influence of the anti-Vietnam war movement, a restless tide of revolutionary anger was catching hold of young people all over the western world. We saw pictures of students fighting the establishment in France, Germany, the United States, and imagined we were seeing the death agony of the decadent capitalist system in the world revolution which would bring in the new age of peace and socialism. In such a world God would have no place and religion, like all other ideas that bound and deceived mankind would be thrown on the rubbish heap of history. I began to feed my mind on communist ideas and the undirected anger and resentment of my adolescence began to crystallise into a burning hatred of the System and a desire to overthrow it by revolution.

I used to go down to a children's playground with a man called Dick, who sometimes visited the Shelter. He was a communist and was dedicated to the cause, giving his all for the people he worked for. He ran this children's playground in Cable Street, Whitechapel. 'These are the people who are going to change the world,' I thought to myself, 'for they are involved where the people are, unlike the Christians who hide themselves behind empty rituals, prayers and are afraid to face the world'.

Yet communism had its other face. I thought of Josef Stalin, the KGB, the Berlin Wall, the Soviet invasion of Czechoslovakia. But of course our communism would be different. It would bring not a dictatorship but freedom. At this time I began also to think seriously about the validity of the work I was doing at the Shelter. An Irishman, Paddy, who had formed a strong attachment to me became ill and was taken to hospital. It was essential for him to stop drinking if he was to survive any longer. There began the painful process of 'drying'. It involved a great deal of time on my part too, to talk with him through the period of temptation, to encourage him in his efforts. Then one day I found him sitting with a half empty bottle of cider in front of him. He looked up at me and said guiltily, 'Our Lord drank wine'.

I felt crushed and defeated. It was not the relapse which broke me as much as the realisation that I had nothing to fill the void within Paddy which would give him purpose and hope in life. At this point the revolution would hardly help, as he would not understand my ideas and philosophy. Within a week I had left the Shelter and retreated back to my parent's home. A dark time, of disappointment and also humiliation followed. I was in revolt against my parents' way of life and yet now totally dependent on their charity. They too were disappointed in me but there was no way to make them able to understand my feelings.

Eventually I decided to teach. At Paddy's age, it is too late; therefore reach them when they are young. I applied for a job in Retford, Nottingham. After the initial teething troubles things began to improve, I had a good relationship with the pupils who appreciated the fact that I tried to make my lessons relevant and interesting, and also that I was willing to take time to talk with them outside lesson time. My age and yet wide experience thanks to travels around Europe and work in the Simon community helped to bridge the gap. I was given the bottom stream of the 5th form and managed to communicate with them, whereas normally they had been considered the malcontents of the entire school. Good friendships with the boys were developing. But still there were deep questions of purpose unanswered within me. I was doing a socially useful job with a reasonable degree of success, but many of the boys' queries I found difficult to answer to my own satisfaction. A further source of irritation was the presence in my A-level class of two Pentecostal Christian pupils who were particularly forthright in their presentation of Christ at every opportunity. Occasionally we would hold long discussions on the relevancy of the Christian ideology.

During my second term at Retford I became restless again. The small market town atmosphere of Retford was not the place I could settle down in. I moved back to London, taking a fresh teaching post in Hounslow at a large comprehensive school. I also knew that there were radical teachers working in London and I hoped to be able to become more involved in the left-wing scene there. Preparation for my changing circumstances came at a Work Camp organised by the Quakers at Sheffield. There were eight British, eight Americans, and eight from the Soviet Union at the camp. The idea of the exercise was to discuss social and political themes as well as to work at redecorating a youth club. I declared that I was a communist at the beginning of the camp, though at that stage I could not really call myself one. I was still ignorant of communist ideology, as I later found out.

As the camp proceeded I found myself becoming the spokesman for the revolutionary opinion amongst the British and American delegations. Although it was organised by a

Christian organisation, the programme of the camp was heavily slanted towards Marxist indoctrination. There were visits to steel mills and coal mines followed by discussion with local trade unionists who just happened to be communists. The soviet delegates were able spokesmen for the superiority of communism over capitalism and explained the reasons for the contradictions and problems of our society by the fact that the means of production (factories, agriculture) are owned by the bourgeoisie and the workers are exploited for profit, whereas under socialism they are owned by the people and used for the good of all. Of course there were strong criticisms of the Soviet Union voiced by many in the Western delegations and I joined in the condemnation of the Soviet invasion of Czechoslovakia and the activities of the KGB. In fact I was not really impressed by the pro-soviet propaganda the Russians came out with and had strong misgivings about the truth of what they were saying from time to time.

However, the doctrine of Marxism-Leninism suddenly came home to me and it fascinated me. It had an analysis of what was wrong with the world: the capitalist organisation of labour and production. It offered a solution: the destruction of capitalism by revolution and the reorganisation of society under the working class for the benefit of the majority, not the minority. What was more it claimed that its victory was inevitable: Marx had analysed the laws governing human history and proved by science and reason that the ultimate goal of history is the establishment of world communism. I noticed the contrast with the Christianity explained to me of late by the Pentecostal pupils. They spoke of being different from others through repentance; Marx was calling one to strive to become like the majority, the working class, and to merge one's interest and identity with theirs and thus unite the human race.

'Tony, do you believe in God?' The question came this time from Lara, the most beautiful of the Russian girls, one afternoon. She was openly flirting with me and I was beginning to feel that I had made a conquest here. 'I am not sure. Sometimes I wonder. You know I think that there might be a God'. 'How can you think such a stupid thing? In our country only the very old people believe in God. We have no need for God. It's just an invention to fool people into accepting their conditions. If you want to serve the revolution you must get rid of all ideas about God.' 'Do you think so?' 'Yes, I know it,' She squeezed my hand. 'Tony, you could do a great deal for the people of the world. Work to make your country communist. Then we will be able to unite the world in peace. Don't be discouraged by the difficulty of the task. Look at the life of Lenin. Follow his example.'

A surge of warmth and pride swept over me. Was this the destiny for which I had been chosen? Was this the reason for my rebellion, my questioning, my searching? A few days later I sat alone in a park in Sheffield, renounced all religion and committed myself to the revolution in Great Britain. Before the camp ended one of the Russian men invited me into his room to drink some vodka. He gave me books about the Russian revolution and encouraged me to join the Communist Party and read the *Morning Star*. He also gave me a record of the Red Army singing Russian songs. There was one song which really gripped me, which he told me was written at the time of the Nazi invasion of the Soviet Union to rally the people. As I heard it I saw in my imagination the progressive people of the world marching to battle with the dark forces of reaction and fascism, towards the bright dawn of a Socialist world.

There now began a time of real change in my life and my thinking which became more and more anti-system and anti-God. It was the system which had made the world such a mess and which had caused people to be isolated from each other and had made life in the cities so unbearable. What was needed was to tear down the old order and rebuild according to new standards and concepts. I began to read Marx and Lenin and to try to model my thoughts on society and revolution upon them, and to apply their ideas to my present situation. I read Marx's *'Wage, Labour and Capital'* and began to understand the economic structure of capitalism by which the worker became a 'wage slave' of capital, selling his labour to the exploiters who profited themselves from his work while keeping him in the poorest conditions possible, and preventing him from reaping the full benefit from his work.

The whole propaganda effort of the system through education, mass media and above all religion was designed to prevent the worker from seeing this truth, make him accept his station in life uncritically and reject the socialist alternative to capitalism.

Lenin's *'Socialism and religion'* argued powerfully against the reactionary role of the Church in fooling the workers with delusory promises about heaven to make them content with their present situation and passive in the face of injustice. Lenin spelled out clearly the need for the 'class conscious proletariat' to reject all religious ideas and spread atheism.

The *Communist Manifesto* showed me how confident the communists were of the inevitability of their victory and that once the worker was enlightened as to the reality of his deception by the capitalist, he would throw off the shackles of capitalism by revolution, join forces with the mass movements of the working class and build the new social order under the leadership of the communist party. This was all very exciting to me. I began to see my potential as an individual serving the masses of humanity, guiding them into the way of peace and progress, interpreting the world in a Marxist way, stripping away the deceptions of the system and building up the revolutionary potential of the masses.

As a teacher I realized the position of influence I held and my lively imagination soon began to devise ways of introducing revolutionary propaganda into my English lessons. Discussions on subjects like the Vietnam war, racialism, the monarchy could be directed onto the evils of capitalism and the need for a new social order. One could contact pupils who were politically conscious and alienated from the system and encourage them to set up radical cells in the school and begin to undermine the system from within. The possibilities were endless. Of course the reality was very different. Most of my pupils were far more interested in pop music, football and boy-girl friends than politics. The large number of Indian pupils whom I thought would welcome my socialist ideas were suspicious and indifferent and I discovered that the aim of most of them was to get on with the system as well as they could rather than to change it.

Discipline too was more difficult in this London school. My

funny ideas about revolution only made me fairer game for
them than the other teachers. They were not impressed by my
progressive ideas. The white pupils were further incensed
against me because I dared to stand up for the Indians and try
to counter their racial prejudice. My arguments about racialism being used by the capitalists to divide the working class
fell on stony ground.

This experience showed me that I needed to be involved
with other like-minded people and that I could not make a
revolution on my own. For some reason I held back from
actually joining the Communist Party. I had however gone
along to lectures at London University on world revolution at
which I met several radical students, many of whom were as
critical of the Communist Party of Great Britain and the
Soviet Union as they were of the capitalist system. One friend
I made, Micky, a West Indian Maoist, was scornful of the
'armchair revolutionaries' of the West. I was becoming
particularly interested in liberation movements in the third
world and was beginning to wonder whether the working
class in Britain and Western Europe was too prosperous and
comfortable under capitalism to risk all in a revolution.
Should we not be looking to the 'wretched of the world' to
make the revolution? Micky influenced me to read books by
Franz Fanon and Che Guevara and to identify more and more
with the downtrodden peoples of Asia, Africa and Latin
America.

These books fascinated and terrified me at the same time. I
began to learn the meaning of 'Imperialism' from the
communist point of view; how the wealthy nations of the
West had plundered their colonies in order to increase the
standard of living of their own proletariat and thus prevent
them from rebelling against capitalist inequalities, at the
same time causing the crushing poverty of the underdeveloped world. I became haunted by the guilt complex of
many white Europeans and even more uneasy in my own
white skin. Yet the hatred and violence of Fanon and Guevara
terrified me. In *'Venceremos'* I read: 'Hatred as an element of
the struggle; a relentless hatred of the enemy, impelling us
over and beyond the natural limitations that man is heir to
and transforming him into an effective, violent, selective and

cold killing machine. Our soldiers must be thus; a people without hatred cannot vanquish a brutal enemy' — (*Message to the Tri-continental*). I was not sure whether this was the way I saw the world being transformed. I wanted a better world not a mass graveyard. But my friends' objection to this was 'These are the people who made the revolution. Not the armchair intellectuals who sit and talk about creating a better world. The capitalist isn't going to give up his power because we ask him to. It has got to be taken by force.'

I saw the logic of his argument, but I could not overcome my fears. There followed a time of moral and spiritual disintegration in my life. I hated the enemies of the revolution and saw no moral duty to keep their rules, whether it was a matter of paying my fares on the Underground or keeping up their moral standard.

Even throughout this period the idea of God still haunted my conscience. Marxism did not condemn any of my actions, and I was a Marxist, so why worry about God? Marxism itself was concerned with politics and economics, not with personal relationships. I felt that the family was a bourgeois institution to be undermined. Nevertheless I did what was probably the worst thing to do from my Marxist position. I shared my guilt feelings and the nagging sense of God with one of my ex-pupils who had first impressed me with his faith in Retford.

Being told of God's love and forgiveness in Christ only enhanced my problem. I threw myself back into the revolutionary cause, in an attempt to forget the suffering incurred. It was a time when there were several demonstrations going on about Vietnam and South Africa. I was caught up in one demonstration at Twickenham in which we actually stormed the local police station to protest at the arrest of several of our fellow demonstrators. The next day I attended a demonstration outside the American Embassy about Vietnam. I found myself standing right at the front holding a picture of Ho Chi Min, when a girl thrust a leaflet into my hand. Not an unusual occurrence in a demonstration but somehow this was different. I read the contents. It compared the attitudes to revolution of Marx and Christ. One said that the fault of man lies with the system, but the other that it lies with man's own heart. 'Change the heart', Christ said, 'and the system will change.' The leaflet threatened me. It made sense.

The next school day I received some encouragement in my revolutionary endeavours through the fact that two of the pupils began to take my socialist ideas seriously. They were impressed too by my involvement at Twickenham on the Saturday. I spent the whole of break that day talking to them of the cause. The headmaster noticed that I should have been present at a staff meeting. He dressed me down for my absence in front of the whole class. I felt persecuted for my beliefs. What was more important, to attend a stuffy staff meeting or to win boys over to the communist cause? The situation grew worse at the school, for whilst I was becoming more and more involved in the revolution my own personal discipline was being reduced to a shambles. I decided to leave teaching and had the idea of travelling to South America to see the revolution in process. Another thought was that I should get direct experience of working class life by becoming a factory worker. I was clearly confused.

At about this time I read a book which served to undermine much of my Marxist teaching. It was *'The new class'* by Milovan Djilas, a Yugoslavian Communist who fought with Tito to bring communism to power, then fell from grace for criticising the way the party ruled after it had seized power. His main theme was the way the communist Party transformed itself from the party of the oppressed into the new ruling class, seizing power, wealth and privilege as it did so. Djilas wrote: 'Party members feel that authority, that control over property, brings with it the privileges of this world. Consequently, unscrupulous ambition, duplicity, toadying and jealousy inevitably increase. Careerism and an ever expanding bureaucracy are the incurable disease of Communism. Because the communists have transformed themselves into owners and because the road to power and to material privileges is open only through devotion to the party unscrupulous ambition must become one of the main ways of life and one of the main methods for the development of communism ... In communism, careerism and unscrupulous ambition testify to the fact that there is an *irresistible drive* towards ownership and the privileges that accompany the administration of material goods and men'.

The inner struggle created within me by Djilas' words combining with my own self doubts in the value of the revolutionary way and with the piercing statement of the leaflet given to me at the Vietnam rally, came to a climax. What was this 'irresistible drive' of which Djilas spoke? Was it the reality of human sin and selfishness which the leaflet I had received at the demonstration claimed to be the root of evil? Did not Djilas's realistic analysis of the situation in Eastern Europe point to the truth of the Christian diagnosis of what is wrong with the world rather than the Marxist one?

Christianity, it seemed, presented me with an equally radical alternative to my waning socialist ideas, namely a Jesus who from within my life would lead me on to a transformation first of my own life and to that of the world. His solution answered all the questions of my past, including the sense of hopelessness before a dying tramp and the lack of moral courage within an immoral society. The claims of Marxism were paled into utter insigificance. In Christ I was to become a new man, with a new nature and a new direction. I now believe that this too is the only hope for socialism.

There is a beautiful ideal in socialism that people should work together for each other's good, but it needs people like Jesus to carry it through. The block is within ourselves, as Jesus himself said:

> It is the thought-life that pollutes. For from within, out of man's heart come evil thoughts of lust, theft, murder, adultery, wanting what belongs to others, wickedness, deceit, lewdness, envy, slander, pride and all other folly. All these vile things come from within; they are what pollute you and make you unfit for God (Mk.8:20–23).

Many people, particularly Western intellectuals, are looking for 'Socialism with a human face', socialism but without the barbarities of the Soviet system. I suggest that the 'human face' is the very problem of socialism and capitalism, and that our contemporary social and political systems reflect vividly the truth of this analysis of human nature by Jesus. The problem of Marxism is that it ignores the spiritual realities of human sin, the existence of God and the existence of Satan.

Most contemporary intellectuals ridicule the idea of there being a personalised force of evil.

By fighting Christianity and proclaiming itself the party of atheism the communist party leaves man enslaved by the power of darkness that rules this present age and so has brought no deliverance to the world but has simply imposed a different form of spiritual and political tyranny in place of the one it removed. Jesus said, 'You shall know the truth and the truth shall set you free.' When we honestly face the reality of our condition and follow Jesus we can find true liberation. What is needed is not 'socialism with a human face' but *'socialism with a divine face'*, the face of Christ leading us in the way of humility, self sacrifice and love. We are living in a day of great disillusion and despair. Many are looking for the answer in politics, education and material prosperity. For some communism sums up that searching. The alternative, however, is Christ.

Notes

NOTES TO CHAPTER ONE

1. 'Religious Education in Secondary Schools': Schools Council Working Paper No. 36.
2. Sidgwick & Jackson, London, 1972, p. 36.
3. *The age of the Democratic Revolution*. R.R. Palme: Vol 2, 1964, p. 128.
4. Penguin, p 174.
5. Penguin, p 13.
6. *Religion and the Rise of Capitalism*, pp 112, 129.
7. Christian Journals Limited, Belfast, pp 83–4.
8. *Kleine okonomische Schriften*, Marx-Engels; Dietz-Verlag, Berlin, 1955, p 139.
9. op. cit. p 149.
10. 'Perpetual Serfdom', Bernard Levin, 13 December, 1977.
11. 'Childhood in China', Lesley and Peter Adamson, December 1977.
12. *Pedagogy of the Oppressed*, Penguin, pp 66, 75.
13. Hodder & Stoughton, London, 1976, pp 15–6.
14. See *The Marxists*, C. Wright Mills, Penguin, p. 451.
15. Wyvern Books, London, 1959, p. 207.

NOTES TO CHAPTER FOUR

1. Tosi del X Congresso: Roma, Editorii, 1963: 666.
2. *Red Star Over China,* p. 148 Random House, 1968.
3. In his essay 'From Commitment to Cant: The Evolving Functions of Ideology in the Revolutionary Process. *Ideology and
   Politics in Contemporary China,* Univ. Of Washington Press,
   1973, p. 140.
4. *Mao,* Prentice-hall, New Jersey P8.
5. *Marx in His Own Words,* Ernst Fischer, Penguin, 1973; 17.
6. *History of the Chinese Communist Party, 1921–49,* J. Guillerman,
   Methuen & Co., London, 1972: p. 19.
7. *Mao Tse-tung* Penguin: p. 127.
8. 'Modernisation and the Maoist Vision — Some Reflections on
   Chinese Communist Goals': *China Under Mao: Politics Takes
   Command,* ed. Roderick MacFarquhar, pp 3 ff.
9. *Religious Policy and Practice in Communist China:* Hodder &
   Stougton, London, 1972.
10. Pall Mall Press, London, 1970, pp. 154–5.
11. *Mao Tse-tung* op. cit. p. 267.
12. *Ideology and Practice,* p. 185.
13. *Socialist Upsurge in the Countryside,* pp. 159–60.
14. *Mao Tse-tung,* pp. 233–4.
15. 'The Fall of Chairman Mao', *Current Scene,* VI, 10: June 15, 1968.
16. 'The Deification of Mao, *Saturday Review,* Sept. 19, 1970, p. 25.
17. Nos. 35, 37, 39, 41: 1966.
18. Hellungkiang Radio 23 May 1968.
19. *Revolutionary Immortality: May Tse-tung and the Cultural Re-
    volution:* Alfred A Knopf, New York, 1968.
20. Univ. of Washington Press, 1973, pp 19–23.

NOTES TO CHAPTER FIVE

1. Camilo Torres: 'Message to Christians' published in *A Reader in
   Political Theology,* ed. Alistair Kee (SCM 1974) p 144
2. Sir Frederick Catherwood: *A Better Way* (IVP 1975) p 109
3. Jose Miguez Bonino: *Revolutionary Theology* p 26
4. Christian Lalive D'Epinay: *Haven of the Masses* (Lutterworth
   1969)

5. *Time* (March 25 1974) p 16
6. Jose Miguez Bonino: *Revolutionary Theology* p 28
7. Jose Miguez Bonino: *Revolutionary Theology* p 23. For a full scale treatment of the economic issues, Andrew Kirk recommends a book I have not yet read: Andre Gundar Frank *Capitalism and Underdevelopment in Latin America* (Penguin Latin American Library 1971)
8. Jose Miguez Bonino: *Christians and Marxists* p 115
9. E.F. Schumacher: *Small is Beautiful* (ABACUS Books 1973)
10. J.M. Keynes: quoted by E.F. Schumacher *op. cit.* p. 24
11. R.H. Tawney: quoted by E.F. Schumacher *op. cit.* p. 219
12. I am specially indebted to Andrew Kirk for his articles 'The meaning of man in the debate between Christianity and Marxism' *Themelios* Spring and Summer 1976, Volume 1, Nos 2 and 3. His comments on the whole of this article have also been most valuable.
13. Exodus 1:11–14; 5:4–19; Jeremiah 22:13–17; Amos 2:6–7
14. See Donald Hay: *A Christian Critique of Capitalism* (Cove Books 1975)
15. Proverbs 21:25–26; 24:30–34.
16. John 7:17.
17. Eph. 2:14–22
18. Gal. 3:22
19. Luke 4:18
20. See Isaiah 35:3–6; Jeremiah 31:31–4; Joel 2:28–29; Ezekiel 36:24–29; Ch. 34; Daniel 12:2–3; Isaiah 26:19.
21. Luke 11:20–22
22. Luke 7:12
23. Romans 6
24. Donald Hay: *A Christian Critique of Capitalism* (Grove Books) Chapters 2 and 3
25. E.F. Schumacher 'Small is Beautiful' (ABACUS) Chapter 17–19 esp. p. 229
26. Isaiah 1:14, 17
27. John 7:49
28. Mark 10: 42–45
29. From an unpublished thesis presented to the University of London: 'The Theology of Liberation in Latin America since 1965: an examination of its biblical base in the Roman Catholic Church'

NOTES TO CHAPTER SIX

1. An earlier and briefer version of this chapter appeared as 'Approaching Marx' in *Third Way*, 6th October 1977
2. We cannot go into this question here. An accurate guide, however, is McLellan, 1975. See also my *Karl Marx: A Christian Appreciation of his Life and Thought*, Tring, Lion, 1979.
3. Miguéz Bonino, however, seems to be legislating for others — making the whole world look like South America. *Christians and Marxists* is rather an ethnocentric view of Christian-Marxist dialogue.